TUDOR CITY

TUDOR CITY

Manhattan's Historic Residential Enclave

LAWRENCE R. SAMUEL | *with Photographs by Piero Ribelli*

THE
History
PRESS

Published by The History Press
Charleston, SC
www.historypress.com

Copyright © 2019 by Lawrence R. Samuel
All rights reserved

Cover image is hand-colored postcard of Tudor City's south park, circa 1930s.

First published 2019

Manufactured in the United States

ISBN 9781467143929

Library of Congress Control Number: 2019945091

CONTENTS

INTRODUCTION

Its popularity with New Yorkers has not faltered over the decades.
−Tudor City Historic District Designation Report, *1988*

The next time you're in New York City, walk east a few blocks from Grand Central Station along 42nd Street, take the stairs near the Church of the Covenant and *voila*!—you've entered another world. Tudor City—the five-acre faux medieval village, albeit with high-rise apartment buildings—is on the far east side of midtown Manhattan between First and Second Avenues and 40th and 43rd Streets, right around the corner from the United Nations. Tudor City is not just the architectural masterpiece created by real estate developer Fred F. French and the first residential skyscraper complex in the world; it's a unique community that has played a significant role in the history of New York City over nearly the past century. The story of the "city within a city," as it quickly became known, tells us much about life in Manhattan since the late 1920s, when the development came into being.

Beyond its sheer size—immense for its time—Tudor City set a pattern for urban residential development by creating from scratch what was designed to be an essentially self-sustaining community. While other neighborhoods in Manhattan had been recently gentrified, none rivaled the scope and magnitude of Tudor City and its grand ambition to offer residents a refuge from intensifying urbanization. Additionally, the ways in which money was raised to build Tudor City were unprecedented in the 1920s, and this also made the complex an important milestone in the history of real estate development. Tudor City has not only served as a key site of New York City (and New York State) history but, even more importantly, has also been a major part of the lives of the many thousands of people (including myself) who have spent time there. Telling the full story of Tudor City thus reveals fascinating, largely unknown insights about New York City and about real-life individuals who have called the place home through the decades right up to today.

Not surprisingly, much of the story of *Tudor City* revolves around the value of land in New York City. Real estate in Manhattan is a universe unto its own, as any New Yorker can (and will) tell you, with the land under Tudor City no exception. The area served as a much-contested site in the 1970s and 1980s, with developers and preservationists fiercely battling it out on the streets and in the courts. A notable cast of characters—including Governor Nelson Rockefeller, Mayor John Lindsay and Representative Ed Koch—entered the fray, with developer extraordinaire Harry Helmsley ably playing the role of villain. (His rival in real estate, one Donald J. Trump, makes a cameo appearance.) Most notably, perhaps, Tudor City was an early example of urban renewal, Garden City Planning and new urbanism, a big reason why it was named a historic district by the city's Landmarks Preservation Commission in 1988. For years to come, Tudor City would serve as a major influence in architecture and design across the country (the commission even deemed it "prophetic") and presage the recent movement toward more walkable and greener communities. "Tudor City is a landmark in New York's physical history," Eugene Rachlis and John E. Marqusee noted in their 1963 *The Land Lords*, having "spurred one of the most dramatic shifts in the direction of the city."[1]

In some ways, the history of Tudor City can be viewed as a microcosm of the history of New York City itself. As the city went through the normal highs and lows of the economic cycle, so did Tudor City; the development's occupancy rate and rent prices (and later co-op values) were directly tied to the relative health of the local housing market. The key economic, political and social factors that shaped the nation in the twentieth century—most notably the Great Depression, World War II, the Cold War and the fiscal crisis of the 1970s—were also instrumental in steering the course of Tudor City. While thus an urban oasis, a sanctuary in the storm that was New York City, Tudor City was at the same time indelibly connected to events taking place in the city, the nation and often the world.

To that point, one major theme that emerges in the telling of the story of Tudor City is the efforts taken by its residents to protect the community from outside forces that were perceived as a threat. From the very beginnings of the development, in fact, those who chose Tudor City as a place to live were keenly aware of the specialness of the community, specifically how it was not just a city within a city but a kind of island on an island.[2] Starting with the arrival of the United Nations around midcentury through the end of the reign of Harry Helmsley in the mid-1980s, tenants waged an almost continual battle to preserve the character and, sometimes, the very land underneath Tudor City. Residents, especially members of the Tudor City Tenants Association, led by John McKean, were a feisty bunch and not afraid to go head to head with whomever was attempting to take something away from the community or alter its unique chemistry. Because of its insulation, it was easy to see why the rich and powerful considered expanding it, establishing residence right next to it and perhaps even acquiring it for their own purposes. The fear that something vastly bigger and more modern would spring up in the shadow of Tudor City was a persistent one, fueling the activist spirit that was and remains an integral part of the community's DNA.

The willingness for a band of Davids to take on Goliaths was the most extreme evidence of the strong communitarian nature of Tudor City. Although in the big scheme of things the stakes cannot be said to have been large—most often the fate of a pair of small parks—the years of political and legal wrangling brought into high relief some major civic issues (e.g., public versus private interests, progress versus quality of life and development versus preservation). Support for Tudor City was bipartisan, I might add, a wonderful thing to see given today's deeply divided political climate.[3] In some respects, Tudor City blazed the trail of major apartment building complexes in New York City, its years of litigation paying off future dividends by clarifying what developers could and could not do. Noise and air pollution coming from the nearby Con Ed plant were a frequent source of angst for residents but also served as a central rallying point that brought neighbors closer together. Tudor City can be said to have been ahead of its time in this regard as well, anticipating the environmental movement of today and the emergence of "green" politics all around the world.

Tudor City can be said to have been both a vehicle of and response to encroaching modernism. Unchecked growth, both in terms of population and the rise of more and taller buildings, was considered a legitimate crisis in New York City in the 1920s. With Tudor City, and many other developments similar to it, Fred French saw a solution to the problem, with "scientific" planning the basis for a more livable city. Locating home near work might seem obvious today, but this was viewed nearly a century ago as a revolutionary concept that directly challenged the concurrent expansion of the surrounding suburbs. In short, French was in the right place at the right time with the right idea, dangling the carrot of "walk to business" to the rapidly growing number of middle-class, white-collar workers. Like many great successes, it took the confluence of a number of factors—in this case a bold vision, a large tract of land, lots of capital, a high-quality product, a sizable market, a boom economy and, last but not least, a willingness to roll the dice to make it all work. French was already an established figure in the world of New York City real estate when he built Tudor City, but the scale and scope of this venture and the risk involved were entrepreneurism at its best.

An intensive marketing campaign also had much to do with the immediate success of Tudor City. Had he wanted, French probably could have been another David Ogilvy or Leo Burnett, employing cutting-edge advertising techniques to sell his product. His company relied heavily on both public relations and advertising to generate awareness of Tudor City for roughly the first decade of its existence. (The end of the Depression and housing shortage during and after World War II made advertising essentially unnecessary.) Print ads for the development, many of which are discussed in the first two chapters of this book, reveal not just how the company wanted to present Tudor City to the public but also how the company perceived its newest and largest project to date. While ads for Tudor City were produced by the French Company and were designed first and foremost as a sales tool (making them in some sense propaganda), a critical examination of them offers key insight into the public persona of the community and how that changed over time.

With its architectural style recalling the grand estates of the English gentry some three centuries past, Tudor City struck a balance between refinement and comfort, a compelling proposition in an era defined by intense social and cultural change. While Tudor City was on a significantly larger scale, other apartment complexes in New York City, including Hudson View Gardens in Upper Manhattan's Washington Heights, were built in the 1920s in the Neo-Tudor style, making it clear that French was capitalizing on the architectural trend rather than inventing it. Steeped in an Anglo-Saxon vernacular, Tudor City felt familiar and safe for a white middle class concerned by the rising multiculturalism of the city and nation. Indeed, many New Yorkers were happy to see the French Company buying up all the tenements in Prospect Hill, not just because the area was considered dilapidated but because those buildings were occupied by what was considered to be an ethnically diverse underclass. The news that a "slum" would be replaced by an apartment complex designed for white, middle-income renters was celebrated as a prime case study of what would come to be called urban renewal. The development of Tudor City thus went far beyond its architectural achievements, carrying with it an overt subtext steeped in cultural biases related to race, class and ethnicity.[4]

The cultural biases embedded in the firmament of Tudor City went further. One occasionally runs across the word *restricted* in 1920s and 1930s advertisements for Tudor City, a word we can only assume means that African Americans were not allowed to rent there. It is understandably difficult to find official documentation for such in the Fred French Company Records, but the Jim Crow practice was unfortunately not unusual for many apartment buildings in numerous cities across the country between the world wars and for decades after that. (The Queensboro Corporation's apartments in Jackson Heights, which were built around the same time as Tudor City and were aimed at a similar market, were also restricted.) Rather than be formally stated in the deeds or rental agreements, racial restriction was enforced via leasing practices by the French Company, which itself was overwhelmingly if not completely managed by the same kind of people it was trying to attract as tenants (the white professional and managerial class). Jews were also excluded from many apartment complexes between the world wars, including the Tudor-style developments in Jackson Heights and Hudson View Gardens, a reflection of blatant discrimination in many spheres of life toward those who were not of WASP origin. One has to wonder, however, how far this unofficial policy extended and for how long. Were Jewish people or those with certain ethnic backgrounds also part of the French Company restrictions? Did the practice stop after the passage of the Fair Housing Act of 1968? More research needs to be done in this specific case and in the broader area of the long history of discrimination in housing in America that continues to this day.[5]

His company's apparent racist policies notwithstanding, French displayed a keen awareness of how to use the media to promote Tudor City, especially in describing what would one day be called offering consumers "the biggest bang for the buck." While reasonably priced, Tudor City offered a host of amenities that did indeed make renting an apartment in one of the buildings appear like a great value. (Target's current slogan, "Expect More, Pay Less," would have fit in nicely in Tudor City's advertising.) French's previous projects were luxury apartments for the wealthy, making it understandable how he was equipped to create and package a similar (albeit smaller, given the lesser square footage) product aimed at middle-income renters.[6] Sandwiched between the high-class buildings for the city's rich and the tenements for its poor, Tudor City was a brilliant example of market segmentation. Fred French was also consciously selling time, an increasingly precious commodity in the Roaring Twenties—with Tudor City, specifically, the minutes or hours saved every weekday by not having to commute to and from the suburbs. The introduction of Tudor City would have made an excellent case history for the Harvard Business School, with the man's ability to exploit the "4Ps" (product, price, packaging and promotion) to his fullest advantage, something that other marketers could have benefited from.

The sense that Tudor City was not just a city within a city but a suburban town or even rural village carved out in the heart of Manhattan was another strong selling point. A backlash against intensifying urbanism, especially its various social ills, was already well in play by the mid-1920s, making the idea of living in a pastoral and bucolic hamlet that happened to be a short walk to and from one's office a dream come true to many New Yorkers. The invention of a self-contained neighborhood from scratch (replacing the "slums" that had already been there) was quite a remarkable achievement, and its self-sufficiency and autonomy promoted a genuine feeling of kinship. There was always a strong sense of community in Tudor City, as well as a kind of understanding among those who chose to live there that they were in a special place. (Tudor City had a "special character [and a] special historical and aesthetic interest and value," the Landmarks Preservation Commission felt.)[7] During the postwar years, many residents were highly social, with any number of clubs to join and activities in which to engage. (If nothing else, this gave tenants an opportunity to get out of their walk-in closet–like apartments for a while.) If one didn't know any better, a reader of *Tudor City View*, the house magazine published from 1934 to 1969, might think that the community was a country club.

While Tudor City operated most directly within the universe of New York City real estate, it necessarily crossed paths with the political and legal spheres as well. The city's rather arcane zoning laws would come to play a surprisingly important role in the story, as did all levels of the city's (and sometime state's) court system. Alongside this intersection with city hall, Tudor City often interfaced with some of its east midtown architectural kin, notably Grand Central Terminal, the United Nations and the Ford Foundation. The community also attracted the interests of some of the major players on the New York scene in the twentieth century, including Helmsley, a number of mayors and Robert Moses. It was perhaps inevitable that "the Power Broker" would enter the story at some point, the man's tentacles reaching into nearly every nook and cranny of the five boroughs over the course of his long tenure as a public servant.

While most people do not know who Fred Fillmore French was (some may recognize his name from his beautiful, eponymous building on Fifth Avenue and 45th Street in Manhattan), the man was a force of nature during his day. His relatively short life reads like a Horatio Alger story, as he rose from poverty to become one of the most successful and wealthiest real estate developers in New York City in the early decades of the twentieth century. French was born in Manhattan in 1883 and spent his childhood in the Bronx; his family was poor after his father, a cigar maker, died. French won a Pulitzer scholarship that allowed him to attend Horace Mann High School, after which he spent a year at Princeton. From there he went west in search of adventure and, after finding it in ranching and mining, returned to New York, where he took an engineering course at Columbia. Jobless, French was somehow able to borrow $500, which he promptly used to purchase the Bronx house where he lived. From there he was off and running (despite his business partner absconding with the company's funds), using buildings he bought as leverage to develop bigger and more profitable real estate ventures. "You can't overbuild in New York," he said many times, his own experience bearing out the truth of the phrase.[8]

Having created the Fred F. French Companies in 1910 when he was twenty-seven years old, French would over the next two decades build a real estate empire worth about $1 billion in today's money. He, like many businesspeople, would suffer a major reversal of fortune with the market crash and ensuing depression, but his legacy as a superb developer and dealmaker and was by then already ensured. Much of French's positive philosophy was delivered to his employees and stockholders in a newsletter called *The Voice of the Fred French Companies* (later just *The Voice*). What comes through loud and clear is his optimistic and progressive view of life, as well as his determination to motivate others to action. French addressed his salespeople every workday morning, inspiring them to, in his words, "kick down the door," if that's what it took to succeed. The man was also apt to have the door of his own company locked precisely at 9:00 a.m., with no employees able to enter after that.[9]

Integral to French's success was the developer's unique "French Plan," which he had employed in the construction of most of his prior projects. As with the development of eleven previous buildings, ordinary investors had the opportunity to put their money into Tudor City as a means to gain a healthy return in exchange for French to construct the complex very quickly, with tens of thousands of people doing just that. Needless to say, the construction of a dozen high-rise buildings within just a few years required a huge amount of working capital. French raised millions of dollars through mortgages for each building and, with the help of a seventy-five-person sales force, by selling securities in the buildings to investors (typically the general public).[10] On top of or alongside a traditional mortgage (roughly 50 percent of the cost of land and construction), in other words, the company created a corporation for each building and issued stock, with individual investors able to buy contracts from anywhere from $100 to $100,000. The finances of each building, including the collection of rent and paying of expenses, were managed separately, offering investors an ideal combination of limited exposure and the abundant resources of the French Company.[11]

This system of financing construction was at the time nothing short of revolutionary. Investors could reap earnings as long as they held the stock, a concept that went far beyond the standard (and expensive) approach of a developer borrowing a lot of money and paying it back slowly with some interest tacked on. Having created it (in 1921), French was fully aware of his plan's ability to raise a lot of money in a short amount of time and proactively used it as a branding technique (and typically capitalized it in advertising for additional emphasis). It's safe to say that French's policy of rewarding those who put up money for buildings with a share of future profits was indeed novel between the world wars. While his altering of the landscape of New York City would no doubt serve as his greatest legacy, French's innovative method of generating very large sums of capital in a matter of months deservedly earned him a reputation as a financial wizard.

In fact, French was better known on Wall Street for his profit-sharing system than for his building accomplishments, as few developers were willing to offer investors a piece of the action for perpetuity. "The French Company obtains a never-ending stream of millions of dollars of new capital…at a much lower cost than it would if it used the ordinary methods of either mortgage bond issues or long-term first and short-term junior mortgages," wrote John Taylor Boyd Jr. in *Architectural Forum* in 1929 in a three-part series titled "Wall Street Enters the Building Field."[12] French offered additional incentive to potential investors by giving them a share of common stock for each share of preferred stock that they bought (while keeping one additional share of common for his company as profit). After ten years, with money made by all parties, the preferred stock would be bought back by the French Company, leaving it and the public equal partners on a particular building based on the even distribution of common stock.[13] "It was our belief that the people whose money helped to make building enterprises possible should receive, in addition to safety, a fair share of the profits earned," French later recalled, something that worked wonderfully in boom times but, as it would turn out, disastrously in a bust.[14] Despite the implosion of his financing plan in the Depression, it is difficult to overestimate what French envisioned and accomplished during his relatively brief life with Tudor City.

Chapter 1

THE CITY WITHIN A CITY, 1925–1929

Tudor City points the way to a scientific rebuilding of Manhattan.
–first display advertisement for Tudor City, June 22, 1926

In September 1929, an advertisement appeared in the real estate section of the *New York Times* that the newspaper's readers likely found interesting and perhaps odd. Alongside the many ads listing apartments to rent in the typical modern lingo of the day was one whose language seemed strangely out of place. "Today the enemies of a great city, sapping the energy, the vitality, and the happiness of its inhabitants as relentlessly as any foe, are rush and confusion, noise and clangor," the ad began, with readers soon learning that those enemies were "the jostling and crowding of countless thousands on trains and subways." Fortunately, however, there was a sanctuary from this terrible locomotive assault. "There exists within New York a great citadel of quiet in which thousands have already found refuge from the clamor of modern life," the ad continued, that citadel being a place called Tudor City. "No noise from the city at its gates can penetrate," readers are then informed, the even more amazing thing being that this seemingly magical place was located in the middle of Manhattan.[15]

Tudor City, the massive apartment building complex situated on the far east side of mid-Manhattan, had already been home to thousands of New Yorkers for a few years, but that did not take away from the rhetorical power and essential truth of the ad. The community really was a haven from many of the city's less desirable attributes, something more people were discovering when looking for an apartment to rent in town. Tudor City would not just offer its residents peace and quiet but also prove to remake the cultural landscape of New York City by means of its developer's conviction that there could and should be what he called "a new manner of living" within an urban setting. The "city within a city," as Tudor City immediately became known, represented nothing short of a revolution in real estate development, one that still resonates today. The late 1920s marked the beginnings of this revolution and served as the honeymoon period for Tudor City in which virtually everything fell neatly into place for its creator, Fred F. French.

A VAST COMMUNITY SETTLEMENT

The area in which Tudor City would be located had a rich history. After buying the Turtle Bay Farm for $1,500 in 1795, Francis Winthrop built an impressive house called Dutch Hill at what is now East 41st Street and First Avenue. Winthrop called the area Prospect Hill, no doubt inspired by its elevation and vista across the river, and the name stuck. A stone fortress stood at the spot where 42nd Street ended at the East River in colonial days, with excavation of the site suggesting that colonists and redcoats had engaged in battle there. (Historians believed that the British made landfall there in September 1776, after the Battle of Long Island; a Revolutionary War–era Hessian cavalry sword was one artifact uncovered.)[16] Great country estates owned by prominent New York families, including the Winthrops, Kips, De Voors, Beekmans and Brevoorts, lined the river from the late eighteenth century through the early decades of the nineteenth century.[17]

By the Jacksonian era, however, Winthrop's fine house had been turned into a tavern and stagecoach stop on the Old East Post Road, and Prospect Hill had become home to shacks, small farms and squatters. Thousands of Irish immigrants had left Lower Manhattan and taken up residence in the area, attracted by its freewheeling ways that perhaps can be likened to what could be found in the Wild West at the time. The "Rag Gang," a motley crew of thieves who had served time in the Blackwell Island Penitentiary and were now led by the notorious Paddy Corcoran, ran roughshod in the area until the Civil War forced the group to disband.[18] (The gang's headquarters, "Corcoran's Roost," was located on the site of today's Prospect Tower, according to legend.)[19] Cookie-cutter brownstones populated by the city's *arriviste* sprang up soon after that war, but within just a decade or two, the

Looking north from 42nd Street and Second Avenue in 1861. In the Civil War era, this part of Manhattan was decidedly more rural than urban. *Wikimedia Commons.*

area had again lost its luster and was deservedly considered a "shantytown."[20] It would be these now run-down row houses and tenements (many of them having been turned into cheap boardinghouses) that already well-established real estate developer Fred French would purchase and demolish to make space for Tudor City.[21]

Given the sights, sounds and smells to be found in Prospect Hill in the early 1920s, French's vision for that part of Manhattan was nothing short of extraordinary. Slaughterhouses, stockyards, packinghouses and a glue factory lined the East River, and lumber and coal yards and an electric power plant further made the section of the borough one of the ugliest and most odorous. (One can only be reminded of the "valley of ashes" described in F. Scott Fitzgerald's *The Great Gatsby*, which was published precisely when Fred French began work on Tudor City.) French imagined something much different, however, thinking that such riverfront property (with a westward orientation) could be transformed into a residential area as grand as Park Avenue or Riverside Drive. While Tudor City and the blocks surrounding it never achieved such grandeur, French achieved much of what he had dreamed for the neighborhood. Tudor City "has a charm and character missing from New York's newest residential buildings, gives the feeling of belonging to the neighborhood, and is likely to remain the home of some 10,000 people for a long time to

The slaughterhouses that lined the East River would ultimately be torn down to make room for the United Nations campus.

come," Rachlis and Marqusee observed, something that holds true even more a half century later.[22]

It can be said that Tudor City was born when the Fred F. French Company purchased a five-acre tract of land on the east side of mid-Manhattan. After seeing Prospect Hill accompanied by real estate broker Leonard S. Gans, Paine Edson, an employee of French's, convinced his boss that the area had great potential for development.[23] French, who loved walking and did not own an automobile, likely needed little persuading. French was fully aware that automobile traffic had already become a problem in the city and concluded that a fair number of the people who worked in bustling midtown Manhattan would want to live there as well. Before World War I, office buildings in the borough were largely limited to the Wall Street area, but by the mid-1920s, a legitimate business district had sprung up around the newly rebuilt Grand Central Terminal. Even if it were used for just one or two nights a week, keeping an affordable apartment in town was an attractive proposition for harried commuters.[24]

The ability to walk to work would be especially appealing to those who had to take lengthy subway, trolley car, suburban train or ferry rides to reach their offices, he believed, as delays on all were not unusual. Efficiency was the order of the day, after all, and being late to work or in getting home because of an electrical problem on the tracks or some other issue was a major concern for commuters. Many commuters had to make connections, increasing the probability of something going wrong. The spreading of germs, questionable manners and pure physicality frequently encountered on nickel-per-ride subways were other strong selling points for French (who hardly ever rode them himself). Even then, although a transit strike always seemed to be looming and the occasional crash could prove lethal, it was the crowding that all riders could relate to. "Packed like sardines, they stand for thirty minutes every morning and evening in badly ventilated discomfort," one of French's ads would tell such straphangers, appealing to these "poor fish" to live within walking distance of their office so they could "renounce the tin."[25]

It was, however, the flood of affordable Ford Model Ts on the streets of the city that he emphasized in advertising and via a rather sophisticated public relations campaign targeted to white-collar workers. "This building project goes a long way to solve the traffic problem of Manhattan Island," French told a reporter for the *New York Times*, thinking that the best way to solve that problem was to, in his words, "eliminate it [by] establishing living quarters near one's place of business."[26] While French would never solve the traffic problem of Manhattan, his vision of a more walkable and livable city did become a reality, just one of many remarkable things he achieved in his relatively short life.

Importantly, by tucking Tudor City away from the rest of Manhattan, French perceived his latest development as not just a group of fine buildings but the first of what would be a new kind of residential community that would transform the metropolis into a more livable place. "It is the first step in the inevitable rebuilding of Manhattan," a November 1927 ad described Tudor City, this rebuilding to occur "not by individual structures, but by whole neighborhoods." What French termed "a new manner of living"—quiet, green spaces, walkability and a single architectural motif—represented the future of the modern city, he believed, packaging all these elements into what most observers of the scene was indeed the most important building project of its day in New York City.[27] French thus saw himself as not only a great real estate developer and financial genius but also as something much more: the man who would lead the way in remaking the world's capital of commerce into a highly desirable location to call home. French would take every opportunity to add a "sense of place" to Tudor City, anticipating many of the concepts of the new urbanism movement by a full half century.

To its credit, the media of the day recognized that Tudor City represented something new and different and was, without question, instrumental in getting French's message out. Tudor City would be "the largest housing project ever undertaken in mid-Manhattan," the *Times* declared on its front page a week before Christmas Day 1925, correctly predicting that French's boldest venture yet would dramatically transform that part of New York City. Journalists welcomed French's plan to redevelop the ramshackle East

Side waterfront, although at least one had concerns about the scale of his proposed project. "New York is promised—or threatened with, as the event may prove—a vast community settlement overlooking the East River from the high ledge at the foot of Forty-second Street," an editor for the *Times* wrote the very next day, wondering if what arose there would overwhelm the area. Although the footprint of Tudor City was set at four blocks, it was unknown how many stories the group of buildings would penetrate the sky (some were saying as many as thirty). Also unclear was how many people would occupy Tudor City, with estimates ranging anywhere from ten thousand to eighty thousand. Whatever its exact size and population, there was little doubt that Tudor City would dramatically alter the physical landscape of that part of Manhattan. The particular location of Tudor City "makes it impossible that this city should ever be hid," the editor concluded, with anyone viewing Manhattan from the east sure to notice what appeared to be an entire town transplanted from sixteenth-century England and then blown up to immense proportions.[28]

Journalists for other local newspapers were equally enthusiastic when learning about the innovative project. "The decadent section east of Third Ave. is resurrecting," the *New York American* happily reported two days after Christmas 1925, seeing the announced rise of Tudor City as a historic transformation of that part of New York City. "New York has been talking about it for years [and] sociologists and Utopians are still dreaming about it," the newspaper exclaimed, seeing the proposed apartment complex as the key piece for the reclamation of what had once been a fine neighborhood. Additionally, Fred French was best known for his Park Avenue apartments designed for the wealthy, making his declaration that rents at Tudor City would be a half or a third of those truly newsworthy. For French, however, this was just the beginning of what would be a transformation of the modern metropolis, as others began to see the advantages of urbanites living within walking distance of where they worked. "The problem of getting everyone into Manhattan Island by railways, subways, bridges and ferries and hustling them back to the metropolitan environs at night, is going to be too vast a problem for humans to solve," the newspaper described French's vision, which offered a direct challenge to the prevailing view that it was the suburbs, which had blossomed after World War I, that best addressed the city's growing pains.[29]

With Tudor City brilliantly framed by French as the first of what he planned to be a string of self-contained urban communities, the local print media effectively served as enthusiastic salespeople for the company. "The idea is basically right," stated the *New York Sun*, thinking that on a bigger scale the development of large apartment complexes near office buildings could solve "the tenement problem…by standardizing construction as Henry Ford standardized [automobile] production."[30] Many apartment buildings were going up in Manhattan in the mid-1920s, but the reporters understood that Tudor City represented something of a revolution in urban real estate development. "Such an enterprise as that of the French Company combines building with town planning," noted the *New York World*, while the *New York Telegram* went even further by suggesting that Tudor City served as "the sanest, most reasonable and at the same time most scientific effort to solve the upper middle class living problem."[31]

This vision was expressed in various ways via a series of brochures produced internally by the French Company that were intended to attract investors in the Tudor City project as well as to generate publicity. "Tudor City strikes a new and vigorous note in New York's building history," one brochure published in 1926 flatly stated, presenting the community as the logical answer to the problems of commuting. It was true that middle-income office workers were increasingly relocating to the suburbs because of a lack of affordable housing in the city, causing them considerable inconvenience and costing them precious time. "Tudor City will point the way to a solution of this situation by converting a neglected neighborhood within easy walking distance of the central business district into a colony of high class apartments at rents within reach of the average pocketbook," potential investors were told, citing the cheap prices paid for the land and the ongoing "bulk construction" as making the venture possible.[32]

It was the unique geography of Prospect Hill—a high ledge pointing down on First Avenue and the East River—that served as the basis of French's concept grounded in walkability. The area's sharp drop further isolated and protected it from both crosstown and north–south traffic, much like a suburban cul-de-sac.[33] Prospect Hill was thus from a geographic standpoint an ideal spot to situate a group of high-rise buildings that would offer thousands of residents sanctuary from the various transportation woes that plagued the city. Cool breezes from the East River would prove to be another selling point, an important thing in those days before air conditioning was common.[34] Beyond its prime location, a host of amenities—including a two-acre park, a swimming pool, tennis courts, a playground, clubrooms and shops—was to be part of Tudor City, French announced, making the place seem more like a suburban country club than urban apartment complex. As icing on the cake, he made it known that the average yearly rent for an apartment at Tudor City would be a reasonable $500, half of what he was getting from his properties on Park Avenue.[35]

Refreshingly Quiet

As many other ambitious real estate developers knew all too well, the ability to acquire a large area of land without breaking the bank was essential to success. Twenty different structures were initially envisioned to occupy the site, making it necessary to purchase many adjoining lots at affordable prices. French was already in the process of doing just that, having taken title to or signed contracts for almost one hundred different parcels in the four-block area between First and Second Avenues from 41st to 44th Streets. French had commissioned agents from the Joseph Milner Company, led by Gans, to buy as many old brownstone houses and tenements in Prospect Hill as possible, as intense a gobbling up of properties as had likely ever occurred in Manhattan. Keeping French's grand plan under wraps was essential to getting good prices, however, something that the agents were somehow able to do. French had about 200,000 square feet to work with then, enough space to put up his group of buildings intended to house about ten thousand people.[36]

Having acquired dozens of properties on the cheap, much due in part to savvy negotiating and fast cash (the five acres were purchased at an average cost of $23 per square foot), French quickly demolished them to make room for the "high class" buildings targeted to the growing managerial class.[37] French chose the English Tudor style of architecture in order to lend old-world elegance to the project that would cost a whopping $35 million (almost $500 million in today's money). Grand Central Station was conveniently located just a few blocks away, more reason why French's scheme made a lot of sense if the developer could pull it off. If successful, Tudor City would shift the social scene of Manhattan southeast, critics noted at the time, making the complex important not just as a real estate venture but in terms of the cultural geography of the city.[38]

French was well known in the city's real estate community for his more luxurious buildings on Park Avenue, but the remaking of down-and-out Prospect Hill into a desirable neighborhood was quickly becoming the talk of the town. "I consider this the most important development for the midtown section of Manhattan since the Pennsylvania Railroad Company built its station at Thirty-third Street and Seventh Avenue," said J.H. Burton of the Save New York Committee, an organization dedicated to protecting the midtown shopping district (especially Fifth Avenue).[39] The city's garment industry was continuing to migrate north from downtown and literally set up shop, pushing out retailers in the process. Burton and others concerned about the continued encroachment of the "needle trades" were delighted to see new residences going up in midtown rather than garment factories, the prospect of ten thousand additional shoppers in the area being even better news.[40]

Demolition of the many dilapidated buildings French had acquired in the area began quickly. Excavation and foundation work for each new building followed, turning Prospect Hill into a massive construction zone. A twenty-two-story building initially referred to as the Prospect Hill Apartments would go up first, his company announced in June 1926, adding that the whole development would be completed in just about three years. (The building, which included a restaurant for both tenants and guests, was soon renamed Prospect Tower, with two more floors added.) H. Douglas Ives, the man French had handpicked to supervise his company's on-staff architects (and who had previously worked for Cass Gilbert, who had designed the Woolworth Building), envisioned Tudor City as a best-of-both-worlds blend of the old and the new. "The architects have endeavored to reproduce the architectural types of the Elizabethan and Tudor eras, in so far as is compatible with modern engineering," the *New York Times* noted, with limestone and sandstone to be used for the lower floors and reddish-brown brick for the higher ones.[41] Terra cotta (in the style of Sutton Place, a sixteenth-century English country estate) complemented the brick exteriors.[42]

Most importantly, perhaps, all the buildings in Tudor City would share the same architectural style, offering the community a strong sense of unity from a design perspective. A few notable architects had utilized "Tudor Revival" for wealthy clients' large country estates in the early twentieth century, impetus for builders to use it in their suburban developments. The design offered a more comfortable alternative to over-the-top Art Deco, which was making its way into more urban environments as well. Although admittedly anachronistic, the "Old World atmosphere," as French described it, was also intended to buffer the tremendous cultural and social change that was currently sweeping across the United States, especially in New York City, with its dense population of immigrants. "Those who remember and love the old New York are happy at the recoming [*sic*] of life and beauty and wealth to the scene of their old haunts among the gardens, the brooks and the elms," a French Company copywriter poetically penned for a 1928 brochure, tapping into a rising backlash against escalating modernism.[43] Stained-glass and leaded glass windows, some featuring images of New York (and New Amsterdam) history and English birds and flowers, complemented the faux medieval Europe aesthetic, as did architectural elements such as towers, gables, parapets and balustrades.[44] An acre and a half of parks and wide streets would add to this feeling of Tudor City being a kind of suburban enclave within the city, a smart strategy to entice the kind of middle- and upper middle-class commuters French believed would be most attracted to the place.[45]

While the exteriors and lobbies would make residents feel like they were in sixteenth-century England, interiors would be thoroughly twentieth-century America, with the latest home technologies, including electric refrigerators, garbage chutes with incinerators and "radio outlets," to be included in all apartments. (More and more stations were going on the air across the country, making many Americans go positively radio mad.) French was also buying Frigidaires for each apartment in Tudor City (the largest order yet placed in New York City), something that was making executives at the Dayton, Ohio–based company (a subsidiary of General Motors) very happy.[46] Electrical refrigeration had recently become popular, and it was a must that it be offered in any new building labeled as "modern." French asked his engineers to evaluate the various brands of refrigerators and, after they recommended Frigidaire, bought $100,000 worth for Tudor City.[47] (Other large apartment complexes—including Lee Plaza in Detroit, the Schenley Apartments in Pittsburgh, the Seneca in Chicago and the Marshall Field Garden Apartment Homes in Chicago—were also being stocked with Frigidaires.)[48] Elevators, and the more the better, were also essential to state-of-the-art high-rises in the 1920s. The Manor would contain no fewer than eight of them, a convenience designed to further expedite residents' commute to and from their nearby offices.[49]

With the land now cleared for the set of buildings, French promptly placed an order for 10 million face or façade bricks, which was by far the largest such order ever made in New York City. (The previous record holder was the Presbyterian Medical Center in the Bronx, which had used 4 million such bricks.) Consistent with his eye for detail, a conscious decision was made by Ives to select bricks that resembled those common in the Tudor era. For the next few years, millions of bricks would arrive on barges from points south, where they were manufactured, to the Tudor City construction site—a moving of building materials of historic proportions. (The subject of bricks in New York City in the first decades of the twentieth century is a story all its own, with the building boom and rumors of shortages the basis for brick "bootleggers" to enter the highly competitive market with shoddily made products.)[50]

GREATER THAN EVEN WE EXPECTED

By early 1927, what would be Tudor City was indisputably taking shape as the first three buildings came into being. The first column of steel was set in the twenty-two-story, 402-apartment Prospect Tower; construction had begun on the ten-story, 215-apartment Manor; and work was to begin soon on the Cloister. French had raised his total cost estimate to $40 million, but he remained confident that his ambitious project would reap big financial rewards not so far down the road.[51] Plans were quickly filed with the city for a fourth building to stand twenty stories, making it clear that French had every intention to move full-steam ahead with his vision of Tudor City.[52]

French was also not satisfied for his buildings to be finished before showing apartments to potential renters. Even before the first building was complete, French advertised heavily in hopes to have leases signed based just on floor plans. Tudor City would be "a complete small city in the center of New York," one January 1927 ad stated, and "refreshingly quiet" because of the absence of cars in the area. "The only motors entering Tudor City will those of residents and their friends," the ad explained, a compelling proposition to New Yorkers already weary of the loud honking that went on day and night in busier parts of the city.[53] The sound of trucks, especially when going up or down an incline, was especially annoying, as was the noise emanating from the elevated trains along Second, Third, Sixth and Ninth Avenues.[54] The simple ability to get a good night's sleep in Manhattan in the Roaring Twenties was thus as good a reason as any for residents to seek out a quiet neighborhood like Tudor City.[55] "Why not sleep as soundly as you did in the country?" one ad asked readers, advising them that "you can feel that way every morning if you live in Tudor City, the quietest spot on Manhattan Island."[56]

French's original idea to rent apartments for as low as $500 per year had by then disappeared, however. One- and two-room hotel apartments in

Prospect Tower were now being advertised for $800 to $2,050, while one- to four-room housekeeping apartments in the building would rent for $720 to $3,100. For French, a mix of housekeeping apartments (i.e., those including a kitchen) and hotel apartments (those that did not have kitchens, at least legally) offered the best way to appeal to the broadest market possible. Prospect Tower was targeted to "the bachelor of luxurious tastes, young

Prospect Tower, circa 1966. *Library of Congress, Prints and Photographs Division.*

married couples who both go to business, girls who have decided to live together and share expenses, and people of means from near-by suburban communities who appreciate the convenience of having a *pied-à-terre* in town for winter months and theatre-going at any time," according to a French Company brochure.[57] Maid service would be available in such apartments, with laundry service, porter service and room service in all buildings. (The French Company occasionally referred to such workers as "servants" in advertising to accent the degree and quality of service available at Tudor City.)[58] French's apartments on Park Avenue were renting for significantly more because of the prestigious address, however, making those in Tudor City still a relative bargain.[59]

Shield on roof of Prospect Tower. *Library of Congress, Prints and Photographs Division.*

Inscription and sconce on Prospect Tower. The inscription reads, "Designed and constructed by the Fred F. French Company Anno Domini One Thousand Nine hundred Twenty Seven." *Photo by Piero Ribelli.*

Another major difference between Park Avenue and Tudor City was the kind of tenant likely to call each address home. While residents of Park Avenue essentially had to be wealthy because of the high rent, the primary target audience for Tudor City was the burgeoning managerial and professional class. Many of the latter were commuting to and from the city from suburban towns in Westchester, Long Island, New Jersey and Connecticut, a fact that French zeroed in on with the initial advertising for Tudor City. Rent was typically cheaper outside the city, but factoring in the time spent going to and fro had to make one wonder if the savings were actually worth it.[60] "The average time spent by the commuter traveling between his home and business is one hour and a half a day," a February 1927 ad pointed out, this daily ninety minutes adding up to a day and a half per month (or eighteen days per year).[61] French dangled the carrot of walking five minutes to one's office in midtown, knowing that many commuters would bite.[62] (In ads, the average commuting time was soon raised to two hours and the estimated walk to midtown somehow reduced to four minutes.) Fifth Avenue shopping was just a ten-minute walk and the theater district fifteen, more reason to make Tudor City home sweet home.

Business executives, or those who aspired to become one, were considered by the French Company to be especially receptive to the value of living closer to work. Time was money, after all, an adage that businesspeople knew all too well. "You are letting a real economic loss occur in your own life that you would not tolerate in your own business," one ad told white-collar workers, tapping into management's obsession with efficiency and productivity.[63] Even better, faster advancement would be the natural result of having another hour or two in one's workday, the French Company explained, appealing to people in all occupations who were eager to climb the ladder of success by getting promoted and making more money.[64] Having to catch the 5:17 for Westchester was no way to get ahead in the highly competitive corporate culture of the 1920s, another ad made clear, suggesting that an extra hour at the office each day could mean the difference between success and failure.[65]

If expressing a long commute in time wasn't persuasive enough, there was always distance. "Do you travel 7500 miles to business?" a March 1927 asked readers of the *Times*, the number based on the average thirty-miles-per-day commute.[66] The marketing people at the French Company certainly did their homework when conceiving different ways to define the problems suburbanites faced going to and from work. Anyone traveling daily to the Grand Central business district would be "jostled by 1,500,000 people," an ad stated a week later, that number reflecting how many

The Manor, circa 1966, with the parks to the left and the Terrace Restaurant in Prospect Tower to the right. *Library of Congress, Prints and Photographs Division.*

Courtyard at the Manor. *Photo by Piero Ribelli.*

workers passed through the area during rush hour.[67] In June 1927, those who rode crowded subways, trolley cars and trains to work and home were told, "The only time when you're not jostled is when there is no room for anyone to move an inch," although that was something they likely already knew.[68] (About 4 million people had just turned out for the ticker-tape parade celebrating Charles Lindbergh's successful solo flight across the Atlantic, the jostling of mass transportation on that day perhaps the worst ever.) "Modern business demands alert faculties, a fresh, untired mind," the French Company reminded the thousands of mid-level managers jockeying for position, advising them to walk to work in order to be at their "physical and mental best."[69]

Coming across such clever ads, many New Yorkers (some of them reading their newspapers on their daily commute) no doubt strolled over a few blocks east to see for themselves what this city within the city was all about. The steel framework of both Prospect Tower and the Manor was up by the end of April, with the brick façade almost to the top.[70] While the group of buildings continued to be constructed, dozens of leases for apartments in Prospect Tower and the Manor were being signed, a vote of confidence that French naturally found very reassuring. While "bachelors" were primarily targeted for the single-room suites of the former, the latter's one, two-, three- and four-room suites could accommodate a variety of cohabitants. "Here live young married couples who entertain a bit, older people who take life easily, people with children, and girls in groups of two or three who find they can create a desirable background for themselves on what is truly a minimum expenditure when they divide it up," a brochure published a few years later said about the Manor.[71]

With the grounds of what would be Tudor City still literally a construction project, prospective tenants walked on wooden boards over dirt and mud to find the shack-like rental office. Signing a lease purely by looking at floor plans was quite unusual for the times and allowed the French Company to make it known that it was ahead of schedule in renting out apartments in the first two buildings. Soon-to-be tenants could see from the plans that the units were, in fact, comparable to those in Park Avenue buildings and had to conclude that Tudor City was indeed by all measures a good value.[72] By the spring of 1927, more than 100 apartments in Prospect Tower had been rented, with French confident that leases for all 520 units would be signed by the time the building opened its doors in September.[73]

Interest in Tudor City among potential renters continued to build. "Flats in Tudor City are renting rapidly," the *New York Times* told readers of its

Entryway to the Cloister. *Photo by Piero Ribelli.*

Architectural elements of the Cloister. *Library of Congress, Prints and Photographs Division.*

real estate section in late June, with the French Company receiving 250 inquiries per week from people interested in leasing a unit in one of the growing number of buildings. Both the Prospect Tower and the Manor would be completed by September and the Cloister soon after that, with none of the usual delays associated with new construction. A fifth building in Tudor City would be constructed, the company announced, a sign that French's aggressive publicity campaign was working. "Our success is greater than even we expected," gloated William E. Barton, vice-president of the company, noting that business should only get better in the fall, which was at that time the busiest renting season.[74]

A SELF-SUFFICIENT COMMUNITY

Given the money to be made and amusements to be had in New York City in the late 1920s, it was not surprising that real estate developers like Fred French were having no problem renting apartments. It may have been Prohibition, but it took little effort for thirsty Gothamites to find a speakeasy that had wisely stockpiled booze before the Volstead Act went into effect. It was the Jazz Age, of course, and real-life flappers could be found doing the Charleston or foxtrot any night of the week in hundreds of nightclubs. Zeppelins flew over the ever-rising skyline, and a new thing called streetlights were helping to prevent the rising number of Tin Lizzies, Studebakers and Packards from crashing into one another and running over the occasional pedestrian.

Need it be said that entertainment was plentiful and varied in New York in the Roaring Twenties, with Broadway shows (notably the *Ziegfeld Follies*) and motion pictures (sometimes in newly air-conditioned theaters like the Rivoli) being every bit as popular as they are today. Anyone happening to walk into Lindy's, the legendary deli on the Great White Way, in the wee hours of the morning could very well have seen Chico and Groucho Marx yukking it up over their sandwiches.[75] Many were flocking to Coney Island to ride the brand-new Cyclone rollercoaster and others to Yankee Stadium to see Babe Ruth, Lou Gehrig and the rest of "Murderers' Row" crush their opponents (the 1927 team is often considered the best in baseball history). "New York had a hell of a good time during the ten years before the great attrition," Milton Mackaye observed in his 1934 *The Tin Box Parade*, describing in detail how the city went essentially crazy before the market crash put an end to much of the good times.[76]

Fred French and his colleagues were no doubt delighted with what they had accomplished so far. It was clear that Tudor City was becoming seen as a desirable place to live by New York's managerial and professional class even before a single building was completed. Beyond the prime (and quiet) location and excellent value, the planned amenities were doing much to persuade people to seriously consider this new development as a place to live. A private park in the community (the first since Samuel B. Ruggles created one for local residents of Gramercy Park in 1831) was now being developed "in the English manner," Barton could report, with shops and a garage also on the way. "In all," he stated, "Tudor City will be a self-sufficient community," a claim that few if any neighborhoods in the borough of Manhattan could legitimately make.[77] Advertisements for Tudor City occasionally described the development as "independent" and even as a "colony," further establishing it as a community all its own and as a kind of settlement in which a distinct group of people chose to live.[78] Advertising also occasionally used the term "restricted" to characterize Tudor City, a word that must have meant that African Americans were discouraged or outright banned from being able to live there. While not uncommon among landlords at the time, even in northern cities like New York, the redlining of Tudor City by the French Company was indisputably a shameful part of its otherwise upstanding past.

His company's apparent racist policies aside, French was hardly done adding to the allure and uniqueness of Tudor City. A second park reserved exclusively for residents would be added, it was announced, with many tenants able to see it from their windows when not actually in it.[79] Devoting additional and valuable land for a non-revenue-generating property demonstrated that French's commitment to creating an urban paradise was more than good salesmanship. On top of that, creating a proper English-looking park from scratch was not an easy thing to do. Managers of some garden apartment complexes in Jackson Heights and Forest Hills in Queens had recently brought in full-grown trees to make their green spaces appear more mature than they actually were, something French decided to with the two parks in Tudor City.[80]

Helping matters immensely in this regard was a new machine invented by one Harold C. Lewis, a self-described "landscape artist." Anyone who knew anything about horticulture could plant small trees, shrubs or bushes in a garden, but Lewis's contraption allowed for the transplanting of big trees (Norway maples and spruces, notably), instantaneously bringing a country or suburban aesthetic into an urban environment. Much like how the increased urbanization of New York City in the mid-nineteenth century led planners to carve out space for Central Park in Manhattan and Prospect Park in Brooklyn, developers in the Jazz Age recognized the value of nature amid the frenetic construction of more and taller buildings.[81]

As the first tenants moved into Prospect Tower and the Manor in September 1927, French continued to sell Tudor City as hard as ever. The community would the following spring offer lucky residents a miniature eighteen-hole golf course in the new park, his company announced, complete with bunkers, sand traps, a water hazard and illumination at night. "Live here and cut ten to fifteen strokes off your score," an ad that month promised experienced players, telling those curious about the game that "this is the place to begin learning." (Golf, both miniature and on a full-sized course, had recently become a national craze, as middle-class Americans embraced all kinds of sports and entertainment previously reserved for the rich.) A professional golf instructor would also be on hand to offer duffers tips, and tournaments for tenants were going to be arranged. "This is believed to be the first outdoor golf course on Manhattan Island," a rather amazed reporter for the *Times* wrote after receiving the latest press release from the French Company's publicity machine, adding that it was "certainly the first to be made a part of a real estate development in this borough." While the lengths of holes would range from just thirty to sixty feet, the course at Tudor City would be "sporty and good practice," the journalist surmised based on French's clever promotional effort.[82]

Tempting New Yorkers dreaming of the country while in town was clearly working. A total of four hundred leases had been signed for the first two buildings, which translated into a 70 percent occupancy rate, a figure that most developers would have relished at this stage in the rental process. More New Yorkers looking for a new place to live, now knowing that they'd soon be able to walk out their door and be hitting golf balls in a few minutes, were no doubt telling their real estate brokers to put Tudor City on their shortlist.[83] Business executives, doctors and salesmen were among the first few hundred tenants of Prospect Tower and the Manor, some of them perhaps drawn to the place because of the tiny golf course.[84]

Tudor City was now officially in business and, by all measures, an initial success. Prospect Tower and the Manor were 85 percent rented when they opened for occupancy on October 1, 1927, the company proudly announced, claiming that was a percentage "never before equaled in the history of New

York City real estate developments." Even better, perhaps, the stock in the two buildings had been quickly subscribed, with thousands of investors having loaned French millions of dollars over the previous twenty-two months.[85] It was still relatively early in the game, but Fred French decided to exult in his victory. One day earlier, 150 guests arrived in the dining room of the brand-new Prospect Tower for a celebratory luncheon, with speeches made by French, legal consultant Chester W. Cuthell and Victor A. Lersner, president of the Bowery Saving Bank. In his comments, Cuthell (who had been friends with French since they were children) focused not on how Tudor City would likely turn out to be a gold mine for those who had invested money in it but rather how it addressed the serious problem of housing in the city as its population rapidly increased. (With about 8 million people, New York was the most populous city in the world, a title it held until 1965, when it was passed by Tokyo.) Packing ten thousand people into a space of just a few blocks served as a great example of the "community building" that the city needed more of, he told the guests. French, meanwhile, offered a historical overview of the area in which Tudor City was rising, taking considerable pride that Prospect Hill had been "improved" by knocking down the old and putting up the new.[86]

Of course, Tudor City was hardly the only real estate development in the city that was benefiting from the economic boom and growing population. Rentals were strong across all five boroughs, as they generally were on the entire East Coast. Developers, flush with cash, were putting up new buildings from Maine to Florida, part of the mad frenzy driven heavily by corporatization and a continually rising stock market. Land booms and busts had been a part of the American way even before the country was a country, but the expansion taking place in the later 1920s had a tenor all its own. High-quality residences were now being put up not just for the upper class but for the swelling middle class, a shift that French was fully exploiting with Tudor City. Occupancy of Prospect Tower and the Manor was up to 90 percent by Thanksgiving 1927, with French executives expecting them to be full up by New Year's Day.[87]

French was determined to acquire every last one of the remaining properties in the four-block area between First and Second Avenues from 41st to 44th Streets. Over the next few years, his company continued to buy old houses in the area to make room for more high-rise buildings to add to ever-growing Tudor City. While the midtown area of the East Side of Manhattan sprang up, the Yorkville section on the northeast of the borough was experiencing a similar revitalization as Victorian rowhouses were torn down, modernized or upgraded. The Chapin School for Girls had recently opened at 84th Street and East End Avenue, something that was attracting a more well-to-do crowd, and Vincent Astor was in the process of building a fifteen-story apartment house nearby that signaled that the area had officially arrived. Just north of that in Upper Yorkville, the Carl Schurz Park area (quaintly described by the *Times* as "that delightfully picturesque section of Manhattan hitherto little visited by the dwellers in the middle portions of the island") was also being rapidly developed.[88] The Sutton Place area at 57th and 58th Streets on the East Side had become fashionable right after World War I when a syndicate led by the Phipps estate created a cluster of private houses (attracting members of the Vanderbilt and Morgan families) and a few large apartment buildings.[89]

Other flourishing East Side neighborhoods had offered French valuable lessons in his conception of Tudor City. Like Sutton Place, Beekman Hill, along the East River between 49th and 52nd Streets, was developed by a group of investors thinking it would be a good spot to locate apartment houses for the moneyed class. Turtle Bay, between Second and Third Avenues and 47th and 50th Streets, had attracted quite a few actors, authors and other New Yorkers in the public eye, no doubt in part because of its proximity to Times Square and the theater district. But none of these neighborhoods came close to the scale and scope of Tudor City or its consistent, even peculiar architectural style. All-the-rage Art Deco would have obviously been the logical choice to express modernity, but French knew exactly what he was doing in choosing a style that had peaked in popularity a few centuries earlier.[90]

Conceived by Henry Mandel, another real estate mogul of the 1920s, it was the 1,665-apartment London Terrace that could be seen as the nearest analogue to Tudor City. With the strong economy of the latter part of the decade and land in Chelsea relatively affordable, Mandel went on to develop what was the largest single apartment building in New York (and the world) up to that point. By 1929, Mandel possessed the entire city block bordered by Ninth and Tenth Avenues and 23rd and 24th Streets, a rare real estate coup even for the times. (Clement Clark Moore, best known for writing the popular holiday poem "A Visit from St. Nicholas," beginning "'Twas the night before Christmas," had owned the land.) Located directly across from fashionable "Millionaire's Row" and completed in 1931, London Terrace was and remains a truly massive complex, with its central structure consisting of ten adjoining buildings. (Four corner structures were later added.)[91] London Terrace offered "smaller, efficient dwellings in large complexes for white collar employees who wanted to live close to their places of employment," wrote Ed Lewis for 201west16.org, language that could be taken directly out of an ad for Tudor City.[92] Even London Terrace was not as bold as Tudor City, however, as with his development Fred French legitimately believed that he was creating not just an immense apartment complex but a new way of urban living grounded in social and architectural modernity.

EVERY SUBURBAN ADVANTAGE

French may have been forging a new kind of urbanism with Tudor City, but he still had to fill it up with thousands of people who could pay the rent. No other area in Manhattan had yet to be promoted as heavily, with French clearly influenced by the modern principles of advertising that were currently revolutionizing that industry. Tudor City was being presented to the public as the answer to a problem, something that was entirely consistent with the hard sell, "reason why" approach to advertising that was being successfully employed just a few blocks west on Madison Avenue.[93] Tired of the noise and congestion made only worse by the popularity of the automobile, many of the managerial and professional class were fleeing the city for the new suburbs being built in Westchester, Connecticut, Long Island and New Jersey. With plenty of fresh air and sunshine, the suburbs were also generally considered a healthier place to live, this alone being a good reason for many to get out of the "dirty" city. But with Tudor City, the French Company explained, leaving Manhattan was no longer necessary. "With new understanding of city planning problems has come a solution," a September 1928 ad explained, with Tudor City positioned as "a residential section made healthy and pleasant, yet in the heart of the town."[94]

The number and range of problems solved by the arrival of Tudor City seemed limitless. A fair number of those leaving Manhattan for the suburbs likely had mixed feelings about making the move, with quite a few tradeoffs to be made. Those used to the undeniable excitement of urban life felt they had been exiled in their new suburban town, with little or none of the theater, motion picture, opera, museum, shopping and dining experiences they had enjoyed to now be had. Places like the Strand Bookstore, Russian Tea Room, Caffe Reggio and Sardi's had just opened, with nothing like them to be found in White Plains or Greenwich. Going into town on Saturday night for some entertainment now seemed like a major ordeal, and one typically had to leave a show after the first act on a weeknight in order to get home before midnight.

Even worse, there were all kinds of chores to be done with owning a house, some were sadly discovering, with no apartment superintendent or janitor at the ready to shovel the snow off sidewalks, feed coal into the furnace or maintain the landscaping. Last, but hardly least, new suburbanites missed the friends they had abandoned in the city, adding to the sense that one had been sent off to a remote, culturally vacuous location.[95] Romance, too, could be adversely affected by moving to the suburbs. "She's a nice girl but she commutes," went a headline of a September 1929 ad, the woman in question's decision to live outside the city disqualifying her from being courted by proper urban gentlemen (despite her ability to "play the piano and speak excellent French," it should be said).[96]

Fortunately, for those sharing such sentiments, there was Tudor City. In addition to trying to stop those thinking that it would be in their (or, more likely, their family's) best interests to leave Manhattan, the French Company attempted to draw back those who had already made the move. Tudor City "gives you every suburban advantage" without the need for laborious house chores, an October 1928 ad expounded, with a playground for the kids on site and the glamour of Manhattan nightlife literally steps away. (A "competent and watchful attendant" supervised children on the playground so that a parent or maid would not have to.)[97] Peacefulness and convenience were no longer mutually exclusive, French informed new suburbanites. "Tudor City brings the country to Manhattan," the ad told those missing city life, the place being pitched as "a pleasant, rural community" and "a restful suburban village."[98]

The French Company recognized that there was only one major problem with Tudor City: most of the apartments were small, even by 1920s standards. To counter this objection, which likely frequently came up when prospective tenants toured a one- or two-room unit, French made the argument that one didn't require as much space as one thought. "How many rooms do you really need?" one ad asked, suggesting that renters in other buildings could be spending good money on surplus space. Part of the reason prices were low at Tudor City was that there were no unnecessary rooms or hallways, the company explained, with a single square foot not wasted. And by offering apartments with anywhere between one and five rooms, tenants could select the size that precisely fit their needs without having to pay for extra space.[99] Finally, double or twin Murphy beds turned the living rooms of the many one-room apartments into bedrooms, appealing to those no doubt wondering how they were going to squeeze into a space not much larger than a walk-in closet.[100]

While most of the apartments were undeniably small, despite French's efforts to describe them otherwise, it was true that one could likely find one that met one's needs. There were by May 1929 no fewer than 147 different configurations of apartments at Tudor City, in fact, with monthly rents ranging from $65 to $258. French claimed this to be "the greatest assortment" of apartments of any single real estate development in New York City.[101] With such an assortment, an apartment hunter need not spend valuable time and energy looking at buildings from "the Bowery to the Bronx," as French put it, presenting Tudor City as a kind of "one-stop shop" for all one's residential needs. If that were not enough, any apartment could be furnished at a moderate additional charge, quite a convenience for those not wanting to go to the bother and expense of shopping for such things.[102] Furnished apartments were in the "old-colonial style," with comfortable wing chairs, printed draperies, soft sofas, thick rugs, gateleg tables, pewter lamps with shades, chests of drawers and desks with glass shelves. Bathrooms were done with flowered wallpaper, adding to the decidedly traditional (even dowdy) effect.[103]

The Hermitage. *Photo by Piero Ribelli.*

Right: The ziggurat-like Woodstock Tower. *Library of Congress, Prints and Photographs Division.*

Below: Ornamentation on the upper floors of Woodstock Tower. *Library of Congress, Prints and Photographs Division.*

Above: Haddon Hall, Hardwicke Hall and Hatfield House—the "3 H's." *Library of Congress, Prints and Photographs Division.*

Left: Thematic stained-glass windows like this from the Hatfield House are ubiquitous at Tudor City. *Photo by Piero Ribelli.*

With rent money rolling in from the first three buildings to help pay off their mortgages, plans were filed by the French Company to add more apartment houses to Tudor City.[104] The ten-story Hermitage, completed in early 1928, would be the fourth installment in French's grand plan. The twenty-two-story Tudor Tower, designed to "appeal especially to the younger set," opened in May of that year (complete with a coffeehouse on the ground floor), with the thirty-two-story Woodstock Tower, the sixth building, opening in 1929 on 42nd Street.[105] (The latter was the tallest

Entryway to Windsor Tower. *Library of Congress, Prints and Photographs Division.*

apartment building erected up to 1929 in New York City.) Eleven-story Haddon Hall, eleven-story Hardwicke Hall and fifteen-story Hatfield House (each named for an exceptional Elizabethan country house in England) would soon follow, after which came the twenty-two-story Windsor Tower and ten-story Essex House.

Also constructed at this time was the twenty-story Hotel Tudor, which was the only building in Tudor City not intended for yearly rental.[106] Rooms in the hotel were rented by the day or week and were "designed for individuals of modest income, who nevertheless keenly appreciate the advantages of a room and bath entirely to themselves," explained a company brochure.[107] With the Cloister, Hermitage and Haddon Hall, French had the opportunity to appeal to a new and highly profitable target audience: larger families. Along with the Manor, these buildings offered housekeeping apartments of up to five rooms, much more space than the mostly one- and two-room hotel apartments found in Prospect Tower and Tudor Tower. (Five-room apartments included two bedrooms, a living room, a dining room, a kitchen, five closets, two baths and a "maid lavatory.")

By June 1928, the French Company was shifting its promotional mix toward families in order to fill these large apartments, which were renting for

Archway to the Essex House that divides the two sections of the building. *Photo by Piero Ribelli.*

Right: The Tudor Hotel (*center*), circa 1966, with the sign on the roof. *Library of Congress, Prints and Photographs Division.*

Below: Decorative brickwork of the Tudor Hotel (today the Westgate New York City), along with awning for the Three Lions Pub. *Library of Congress, Prints and Photographs Division.*

as much as $2,700 (raised to $3,100 the following month). The company was not above playing on the guilt some husbands likely felt when not making it home in time for dinner with their families in the suburbs. Appealing to wives who felt that their husbands had become strangers because of their long commutes was another persuasive technique. In one ad that month aimed at wives, we see a family of four, sans father, at a dinner table, with an

Tudor Tower (*left*) and Windsor Tower (*right*), circa 1966. *Library of Congress, Prints and Photographs Division.*

Lower floors of Tudor Tower, circa 1966. *Library of Congress, Prints and Photographs Division.*

Bench and stained glass in entryway to Tudor Tower. *Photo by Piero Ribelli.*

empty place setting in front of a vacant chair. "Don't be a train widow," such women are advised, "move to Tudor City."[108]

Much like today, New Yorkers of the 1920s who had the resources were eager to escape the city in the summer (especially given the lack of residential air conditioning at the time). There may have not been the Jitney or Hamptons Express ninety years ago, but many of the upper middle class looked for every opportunity to get out of town on weekends between Memorial Day and Labor Day. With Tudor City's location along a high cliff along the East River, the French Company was aware that it could present the place as a refuge from Manhattan's famous stifling summer heat and heavy air. For these three months, Tudor City was "a summer resort for those who summer in town," a June 1928 ad maintained, an urban alternative to the rented beach or country house. With its cool breezes, green parks and open spaces, Tudor City proved that "even in summer, New York can be a pleasant place to live."[109]

A RICH REWARD

Having had success with his unique financing method in previous projects, French pushed his "French Plan" hard as he built the first units of Tudor City. Readers of the *New York Times* were regularly pitched to invest in a building and, if intrigued, could receive a sixty-four-page booklet called "The Real Estate Investment of the Future" in the mail. (More than 150,000 people had requested a copy by February 1928.)[110] "It should prove the most interesting and profitable half hour's reading you have done in many months," the Fred F. French Investing Company promised.[111] Investing in Tudor City was investing in New York City itself, prospects were told, a smart strategy given the continuing growth of the city and its rising real estate values (a 12 percent increase in 1926).[112] It was unlikely that ordinary investors could become real estate moguls like Fred French (or John Jacob Astor), but they could buy a piece of Manhattan by putting a modest amount of money into one of the Tudor City buildings. Tudor City represented "an investment opportunity for every New Yorker," a November 1926 ad declared, tantalizing readers with the prospect of owning a tiny part of the "capital of the world."[113]

Given the speculative nature of real estate investing, French was sure to make it clear that Tudor City would utilize the same financing plan that was used in no fewer than eleven previous projects (16 Park Avenue, 15 Park Avenue, 17 Park Avenue, 55 Park Avenue, 551 Fifth Avenue, 34 East 51st

Street, 59 East 54th Street, 22 West 77th Street, 1010 Fifth Avenue, 1140 Fifth Avenue and 1160 Fifth Avenue).[114] Interest payments and semiannual dividends on preferred stock had been regularly paid on building projects that had been completed, giving all appearances that, unlike many real estate ventures that had solicited outside investors, the French Plan was not a scam.[115] Those who had invested in 15 Park and 16 Park would receive their second redemption payment of 10 percent on June 1, 1927, more evidence that the plan actually worked.[116]

In fact, with much money needed to be raised because of the number of buildings being put up in Tudor City, the French Company was telling prospects with some extra cash on their hands that its plan had now been "perfected." Although it helped to be a finance major or have professional advice to understand the intricacies of the plan, the method basically offered prospects two ways to invest money in Tudor City. The first was as a bondholder, whereby investors would receive a relatively small fixed return for the use of their money; the second was as an owner-operator, whereby investors would receive all net profits above fixed charges, plus any additional profit due to appreciation and increase in the rental value of the property if it were sold.[117] Either way, the record showed that the French Company had and was continuing to pay investors solid returns, with no reason to suggest that those wanting to own a piece of Manhattan by sharing the cost of building Tudor City would get swindled.

Much of the success of the French Plan had to do with the fact that there was plenty of investor money to be had in the late 1920s. Mackaye recalled how not just wealthy New Yorkers but the middle class were keenly interested in how to turn their nest eggs into bigger ones by smart investing:

The town and the nation were money-mad. Everyone was in the stock market; nursemaids talked in Central Park about Goldman-Sachs and General Foods, busboys eavesdropped on prosperous diners and bought Auburn [a luxury automobile company] for a five-point rise, novelists and lady poets at literary teas cut art dead and talked about their investments. Even the actors, usually content to lose their savings in Los Angeles real estate or a flyer at the track, opened brokerage accounts and abandoned their matinees to watch the ticker tape. Riches became an affliction.[118]

Fred French seized this unprecedented opportunity to borrow money from ordinary people suffering from the affliction to get rich. Thankfully, he had a great story to tell them. With seven buildings up and running by

June 1929 and two more being constructed, it was clear that Tudor City was an unequivocal hit. Management was having no problem renting the units, with some leading society figures choosing to call Tudor City home. Although the rents had been raised over the past two years, they remained reasonable, especially given the location and amenities. Doctors and nurses (described as a "medical bureau") were on staff for residents of the new thirty-two-story Woodstock Tower, for example, with a valet service, private police force and "radio expert" also on site.[119] The Woodstock Tower also offered balconies and terraces with city skyline and river views, making the one-room apartments in the new building feel larger.[120]

Rather than start scrimping on services and amenities to save money, as some developers might have done, French continued to make Tudor City a more desirable place to live. The restaurant in Prospect Tower was charging $1.00 for luncheon and $1.50 for dinner—a relative bargain even in these times—and two additional restaurants (one in Woodstock Tower and the expanded coffeehouse in Tudor Tower) were now on the premises. There was also a garage and a taxi stand for those opting not to utilize Fred French's favorite mode of transportation—walking. The community stores in the lobbies of some buildings were "in direct telephone communications" with one's apartment, meaning tenants could have their deli sandwiches, groceries, newspapers, books or cigarettes waiting for them downstairs or delivered upstairs.[121] Last but not least, the 1,750-room, forty-two-story hotel being built would offer guests the use of a swimming pool, a bowling alley, handball courts and a gym and be open for business in the fall of 1930.[122]

It could not be disputed that French had radically transformed Prospect Hill in a matter of just a few years. By the beginning of the summer of 1929, Tudor City had a population of three thousand, not large by city standards but highly dense given that the residents were stacked on top of one another within a four-block area.[123] With some two thousand apartments to be found within eight buildings by the end of that summer, however, Tudor City could legitimately be considered a "city within a city." There was now a private school for children up to eight years old on the grounds (Miss Traver's Tudor City School) and an indoor playground to complement the one outdoors (overseen by a governess), more reason why families who might otherwise be living in Westchester or Connecticut were staying put in Manhattan.[124] The arrival of the Essex House and its large apartments (up to six rooms) was more good news for parents reluctant about pulling up their urban stakes.[125] Apartments in that building included a separate maid's room, eight closets, a large foyer and an open fireplace.

Perhaps best of all, however, the bedrooms had a separate hallway that eliminated the need to pass through the living room to reach them—very good news for parents (or kids) wanting some privacy.[126]

For Windsor Tower, which would be first occupied on New Year's Day 1930, French decided to offer both economy and luxury. There were hundreds of one- and two-room apartments to rent for sixty-seven and ninety-six dollars per month, respectively, with just one bathroom and a serving pantry squeezed into the small space. On top of the building were a number of special penthouse studio apartments with fireplaces "in deep Elizabethan inglenooks," double-height ceilings and private roof gardens, a first for Tudor City.[127] The three- and four-room duplex studios offered unobstructed views of the river in all directions, no doubt attracting a kind of New Yorker who would otherwise never consider living in rather bourgeois Tudor City.[128] Residents of such apartments (and some lucky others whose smaller but high-floor units faced east) could see "the ever changing panorama of the shipping, the busy commerce of the river, sunrise and sunset gilding the waters," a November 1929 ad poetically promised.[129]

The fact that the stock market had precipitously dropped just a few weeks before that ad was published apparently mattered little to Fred F. French. While French had enjoyed great success with Tudor City since the Prospect Tower's opening two years earlier, it did not slow his efforts to seeking funding from outside investors. Solicitations continued as hard and as frequently as ever, with much money still needed to pay off the buildings' construction loans. Happily, French could tell new potential investors that his company had been steadily paying back the stockholders of both Prospect Tower and the Manor. Investors in each had been regularly receiving their 6 percent semiannual dividend right on schedule, with the first payback of 10 percent of capital to be paid on September 1, 1929, for Prospect Tower and the following month for the Manor. "These early investors are now reaping a rich reward," an ad informed those looking for a place to put some money, with the French Company's track record speaking for itself. "It is already the largest building enterprise in the world in which the public has been admitted to partnership," the company claimed, asking more investors to sign up for its "perfected" French Plan.[130]

While Fred French could look back on the last few years with much satisfaction, Tudor City was on the brink of entering a much different chapter in its history. The full economic impact of the October stock market crash had not yet taken effect, but it would soon, throwing a very large monkey wrench into his "perfected" method of financing his buildings.

Chapter 2

COMING OF AGE, 1930–1945

There is no place like Tudor City.
—advertising theme line for Tudor City

In January 1932, the high school class of 1882 from Public School 28 in Manhattan gathered for its fiftieth reunion at the Hotel Astor. The gray-haired men and women (one of them Supreme Court justice Peter Schmuck) looked back nostalgically "when New York was New York," as the saying went, offering a peek into how much the city had changed over the past half century. Big-as-a-hat ginger cakes, a popular lunch item at the time, sold for a penny, the group fondly remembered, also recalling that the current site of the New York Public Library was then a reservoir. Chasing goats at 42nd Street and Broadway, now the heart of Times Square, was a fun pastime, as was "ducking" (skipping) school on a warm spring day for a dip in the Hudson River. It took most of the day to get to and from Central Park from midtown, they also reminisced, the primary mode of transportation being trolley-pulling horses that were in no particular hurry. Also vividly etched in the minds of these members of the class of '82 was the "shantytown" that existed where Tudor City had recently risen. The shabby row houses were gone, replaced by a dozen tall buildings that were intended to represent the future architectural landscape of Manhattan.[131]

Prospect Hill and virtually all of New York City had indeed been transformed into a much different place since the days of horse and buggies. The advent of subways and motorcars had fundamentally altered the ways by which New Yorkers moved about, and the rise of skyscrapers had and was continuing to literally cement the city's reputation as the business capital of the world. Fred F. French, who was born just a year after the class of '82 graduated, had successfully capitalized on each of these major developments by allowing thousands of New Yorkers to, as it was expressed in his aggressive advertising campaign, "walk to business." While many in the Machine Age celebrated the new and faster methods of transportation, French loathed them—this was the very basis for his decision to offer like-minded urbanites a more pedestrian-friendly alternative. After a remarkable initial run in the late 1920s, Tudor City was about to have quite a different experience during the Depression and World War II years, as powerful economic, social and political forces reshaped the cultural contours of the "city within a city." Tudor City was "coming into age," to paraphrase a journalist, and finding new ways to adapt to a different world.

A SOUND AND CONSERVATIVE METHOD

Although French likely lost a bundle in the October 1929 crash, both personally and professionally, he must have rejoiced in the fact that almost all of Tudor City's construction was now complete and its financing was firmly in place. It was just a few months into what would soon become known as the Great Depression, but as yet there were few signs that the economic crisis was slowing down his efforts to present his development as a suburban paradise that happened to be located in the heart of Manhattan. Those with large holdings of stocks may have been ruined, but Tudor City appeared to be bigger and better than ever. In March 1930, an indoor miniature golf course opened in Windsor Tower, complementing the one across the street in the south park. The three-thousand-square-foot course (a par 41, with synthetic turf, sand traps and water hazards) was on the "D" floor (First Avenue level) of the brand-new building and served as yet another amenity that few if any other apartment complexes in the city or nation could claim.[132]

Indeed, over the first few months of that pivotal year, rentals at Tudor City remained relatively strong, suggesting that many of the managers and professionals who made up the majority of its residents had, for the moment at least, kept their jobs. "The Great Depression came later to New York than it did to the industrial cities of the heartland," Mason B. Williams noted in his *City of Ambition*, although within a few years, significant numbers of white-collar workers in the city would be unemployed.[133] French was advertising the development as heavily as ever, needing a steady stream of revenue in order to pay off the mortgages on the buildings and the more than thirty thousand investors who were fully expecting to receive their 6 percent income and regular dividends. A few months following the crash, with clear signs that the nation's economy was entering not just a long recession but a deep depression, a change in the tone of advertising for both rentals and the French Plan could be detected. "Safety or profits?" an ad just three days into the new decade asked readers of the *New York Times*, with the company explaining that with the French Plan, investors could have both. The issue of safety (i.e., the relative risk of a stock or bond) had never been addressed so directly in communications with the public, a byproduct of the giant egg that Wall Street had laid.[134]

Indeed, it was clearly evident that French understood that his plan offered understandably skittish investors an attractive alternative to the volatile stock market. The French Plan was "a sound and conservative method" of investing, an ad just a week later stated, the tangibility of real estate another plus over most corporate stocks and bonds.[135] As well, French had always presented his company as experts in New York City real estate, but now he emphasized his track record of building and managing income-generating properties. "Success depends upon specialized knowledge and experience," another ad stated, words of comfort perhaps to those looking for a safe place in which to put whatever was left of their nest eggs.[136] In fact, one needn't know a thing about real estate to make money from it, the French Company told prospects, with profits waiting for those willing to put their trust in experts like themselves.[137]

Advertising to attract new tenants had also taken a new approach in recent months. The reasonable rents and array of amenities for Tudor City tenants had always been prominently featured in advertising individually, but now they were presented as a package offering great value for apartment seekers. Luxuries like maid and valet service and a garage were standard at Tudor City, potential renters learned, with a range of other nice perks also available at no additional cost. (A theater ticket agency, a library, radio repair service and ping-pong tables had recently been added.)[138] The fact that there was a governess to watch over children at the indoor playground was by itself a convenient and cost-saving amenity, especially for this era's version of "dual-career" families.[139] Tudor City was ideal for bachelors, too, the company told young single businessmen, with staff members ready to do one's laundry, clean one's apartment, prepare all of one's meals and even offer a few golf pointers.[140]

A fair number of such individuals would soon be going to work in the Chrysler Building that was near completion. The seventy-seven-story, Art

Deco skyscraper, which was located just a few avenues away from Tudor City, was now the world's tallest building, a distinction it would hold for eleven months until its neighbor, the Empire State Building, took that honor. About six weeks before the official opening of the Chrysler Building on May 27, 1930, French directly appealed to businesspeople who would be working there and who were currently commuting to midtown, recalling the original advertising message for Tudor City. "You've given your business a comfortable, convenient home," an ad addressed soon-to-be tenants of the Chrysler Building before asking them, "Will you do the same for yourself?" With Tudor City just a five-minute walk from work, one could go home for lunch or even play the miniature eighteen-hole golf course as a "pleasant break in the day." French also expected business in the two restaurants and coffeehouse, which were open to the public, to pick up with the presence of the huge office building and, perhaps, convert some of those diners to tenants.[141] With money tight, lunch prices at the dining venues remained reasonable: $0.50 (about $7.50 in today's dollars) at the coffeehouse, $0.75 ($11.00) at the Tudor City Restaurant and $1.00 at the Woodstock Restaurant ($15.00).[142]

French looked to attract managers and professionals from other large midtown buildings as part of a more targeted ad campaign in a more challenging rental climate. Workers in the twenty-nine-story Graybar Building who were commuting from the suburbs were prime candidates as Tudor City renters, especially for professionals like architects who never seemed to have enough hours in their days. (That building was completed in 1927, the same year as the first two buildings in Tudor City.) One could turn the living rooms of larger apartments into studies for working in the evenings, an April 1930 ad informed such workaholics, a better alternative to having to stay late at the office, catch a late train, miss dinner and, worst of all, "annoy the cook." Just as work involved the overcoming of obstacles, Tudor City could "solve the problem of your home," the ad explained in the rational, how-to language popular at the time.[143] "You can walk home in a few minutes to a piping hot dinner and a pleasantly surprised wife," another ad advised, a compelling proposition for those whose jobs had taken over their lives.[144]

The new more no-nonsense tone of Tudor City advertising was, of course, entirely consistent with the dire economic straits of the country. A June 1930 simply answered four questions people might have about the apartment complex: What is Tudor City? Why is it a convenient place to live? Why is it a pleasant place to live? Is it expensive?[145] A similar one pointed out its five advantages—this fact-based approach was intended to be, more than anything else, informative.[146] The French Company was fully aware that many if not most people who lived or worked in Manhattan knew something about Tudor City, as it had received considerable media attention as it was built. Getting people to actually see it for themselves remained a primary goal, however, as the company felt it had a good chance of winning many over through the sheer beauty and isolation of the place. "You'll find in Tudor City an environment different from any other part of New York," an August 1930 ad promised, suggesting that people "come over today for luncheon and look around."[147]

ACT NOW

Those doing so would see workmen putting finishing touches on the most recent addition to the complex. On October 1, 1930, the twelfth building in Tudor City opened, with the Hotel Tudor (downsized to about six hundred one- and two-room suites, some with terraces) catering to those liking the development but not interested in committing to an annual lease. Single rooms cost $2.50 per night, and weekly rentals for $14.00 were available as well. Rooms were, again, furnished in early American or Colonial style, with "soft carpeting," and came with a private bath and telephone.[148] In addition to visitors to the city, the hotel was targeted at those who frequently traveled on business or for pleasure, making it for them a *pied-à-terre*. Friends of Tudor City tenants who unexpectedly came to town (or missed the last train to the suburbs) were also invited to stay at the hotel.[149] As a nice plus, all the services of Tudor City were available to guests, providing greater convenience and sense of community than that at a typical hotel.[150]

Exclusive to the hotel, Tudor City now consisted of 2,807 apartments of from one to six rooms each, with 581 French Company employees serving the tenants. Revenues from the hotel would increase Tudor City's total yearly rent income to about $4.5 million, the company estimated, with development costs to date running about $30 million ($10 million less than the last stated estimate).[151] Despite the solid revenues and cost savings, Tudor City was not fully occupied, a situation that the company's management was more determined than ever to rectify. Needing cash quickly in order to pay off its mortgages and investor loans (as well as to fund other building projects), the French Company began after the September 1930 renting season to "adjust" the price of some of its empty apartments, an unprecedented move. A one-room apartment could now be had for just $64, with special rates on some larger ones as well. The renting office was staying open until 9:00 p.m., with managers hoping there would be a few takers among those who drifted in after work.[152]

Naturally, the French Company did not reveal that it was in desperate need of additional cash, spinning the "few" vacancies and discounting as a normal condition of a giant apartment complex like Tudor City. Giving the impression that Tudor City was in bad financial shape could cause panic among its thirty thousand investors, not to mention the bankers who wrote the mortgages. "They are all eminently desirable and offer such obvious values that immediate action is required if you are to take advantage of this offer," an October ad read, urging those in the market to "act now."[153] As well, the company was still pushing its French Plan, trying to get new investors to pump money into its now strained financing method. French boasted of 70 percent room occupancy and "a waiting list for the choicest suites" at the new hotel as a means to present the moneymaking opportunity of his famous plan. Manhattan real estate was "the field that has produced many great fortunes," the company puffed, adding that it was "recognized as a basic investment by every authority on finance."[154] Real estate in general was a sound investment, an ad a week later pointed out, as "everyone must have a place to live, sleep, and call home."[155]

While it was true that real estate, especially that in New York City, was typically a good place to put one's money, these were highly unusual times. The country was showing no signs of pulling out of its economic slump; in fact, the Depression seemed to be getting deeper. Rather than recognize the vacancies as a short-term situation calling for some minor discounting, the French Company appeared to understand by November 1930 that it had to alter its overall marketing strategy with regard to Tudor City. The year 1930 was now "the economy year at Tudor City," according to an ad published a week before Thanksgiving, quite a different story than what French was telling readers at the beginning of the year, when many believed the stock market would soon rebound. Not only that, but Tudor City "was built for economy," the company was now claiming, a bit of revisionist history that overstated its affordability. The saving of time rather than money was the original key selling point of the place, but 1930 was turning out to be a much different year than 1927.[156]

Retaining current tenants was just as important as attracting new ones, if not more so. Although city hall urged landlords to not evict tenants who had lost their jobs, used up their savings and couldn't pay their rent, it was unlikely that the French Company or any other real estate manager would allow residents to live in their apartment buildings free of charge for an extended period of time. Some tenants of more upscale developments like Tudor City were moving to more affordable neighborhoods, sometimes the very ones in which they had previously lived. Fortunately for Fred French, Tudor City and his other, even more high-end properties were better positioned to weather the economic storm than landlords of properties catering to blue-collar workers. For a variety of reasons, New York as a whole was more Depression-proof than other American cities. "Because of the diversity of its economy and the size of its white-collar workforce," wrote Mason B. Williams, "joblessness was nowhere near as catastrophic in the five boroughs as it was in the industrial cities of the Midwest."[157]

With the making and saving of money now many individuals' top priority, the ability to walk to work from Tudor City was presented as a way to economize. "Legs are still the cheapest means of transportation," went the headline of an ad a few weeks before Christmas 1930, with savings to be had that went far beyond a five-cent subway ride. The two hours to be gained by living so close to one's place of business could be considered money in the bank because of the extra time and energy one would have to devote to work.[158] "If you don't walk to business you are extravagant," the headline of an ad published a few days later, was the flipside to this line of thought, with those taking mass transportation or driving to and from work wasting valuable time and precious energy.[159]

While 1930 had turned out to be the "economy year" at Tudor City, 1931 began much the same way. The French Company was now offering monthly "specials," such as a two-room apartment in Prospect Tower for $95 per month.[160] "Make your money go as far as possible," the company told bargain-hunting apartment seekers, citing Tudor City's "22 famous conveniences" as more reason to consider the place as one's next home.[161] Besides the low rent, there were "452 servants to command" at Tudor City, that number referring to the size of the staff ready to be in service to tenants in some way. (About 130 had apparently been laid off over the past six months.)[162] Tenants at Tudor City were overwhelmingly middle class, but living there made one feel rich, the company suggested. While one might live in a $100-per-month apartment, there was a private "million dollar park" for residents, something even the swells on Park Avenue couldn't claim.[163]

As Fred French did everything he could to bump up the occupancy rate of Tudor City so that he could pay his many companies' bills, good fortune came his way. On May 1, 1931, the Empire State Building opened its doors, its 102 floors capable of being filled with thousands of businesspeople likely not living within walking distance. The building was eight blocks and a few avenues farther away from Tudor City than the Chrysler Building, but it was still close enough to attract many potential residents. (Throughout much of the Depression, the building would be nicknamed the "Empty State Building" because of its lack of tenants.) French saw the now tallest building in the world as much more than a business opportunity, however, taking time out from his budget-based advertising campaign to celebrate what he considered to be a major architectural achievement. French saw parallels with his bold attempts to remake the city with the developers of the Empire State Building, taking an ad in the *New York Times* on May 1 to express his thoughts:

> *Today marks another great forward step in the development of our city. And today it seems only fitting that we who have also tried to do our part in building up New York pay tribute to the genius, the courage, the foresight of those great men who are responsible for this newest wonder, not only of New York but of the world as well.*[164]

French also no doubt took comfort in words said the very day before by former New York State governor Al Smith. Much like French, Smith believed that locating large apartment complexes near office buildings would go a long way toward easing the transportation problems of Manhattan. "The solution is in the building near the business centres of residential districts," he said, something that "has been attempted in Tudor City." Besides sharing a similar view with French on urban development, Smith preferred walking to the subway, seeing the former as a means to better health and the latter as something that involved "taking a chance of life and limb."[165] Interestingly, Jimmy Walker, the mayor of New York City, thought likewise. On the advice of his doctor, the mayor lived up to his name by often strolling around the neighborhood near his apartment. "Walk to work and be happy," he told the *New York Evening World*, words that could easily have been spoken by Fred French when he first told the world about Tudor City.[166]

Mr. French's Name

In fact, the mayor's perambulatory advice appeared to reinvigorate French. Seemingly inspired by the grandeur of the Empire State Building and by notable New Yorkers who, like he, preferred to traverse Manhattan by foot, French promptly dropped his fire sale approach of promoting Tudor City. The economy was as bad as ever, but by the spring of 1931, his company had returned to its original marketing platform grounded in the various benefits of walking to work. "How can a chap stick to his job when his mind is full of trains and automobiles, or when the stickiness of subterranean travel lands him at his office thoroughly rumpled in garb and out-of-sorts with the world?" one ad asked readers.[167] In a rare ad targeted to women, a fictional secretary to a company president arrives at work looking neither rumpled nor crumpled, as she was able to walk to the office from her apartment at Tudor City.[168]

By the summer of 1931, French had moved even further away from his brief obsession with economy. A new campaign focused on the friendliness and peacefulness of Tudor City, with its parks, gardens, playgrounds and gracious appearance an antidote to the strife of urban life in the depths of the Depression.[169] The old-world charm of the neighborhood could "not be found elsewhere in New York" and was another reason why Tudor City was unusually pleasant.[170] The residents of the community were also "the kind of people you will be glad to know," with those choosing to live there sharing a spirit not found anywhere else.[171] (Given the French Company's occasional claim in advertising for Tudor City that the community was "restricted," this also could have been code that those people were white.) Tudor City's forty thousand square feet of private parks also had much to do with this unique quality of life, another ad that summer pointed out, with laughing children playing in them and bringing much joy to the place. The parks not only saved mothers a long walk to a public playground but also helped to make children growing up in the city healthier. "The little folks need the out-of-doors, need green grass and sunshine to make them strong and well," as parents with children currently living in other parts of the city (and perhaps considering a move to the suburbs) were told.[172]

It was, however, the death of Fred French that likely had the most impact on the community that he had built. French, who had risen from poverty in childhood to become one of the top real estate developers in the country, reportedly died suddenly in his sleep in August 1936 at age fifty-two from a heart attack.[173] Although he was obviously a wealthy man, French's will revealed that he had less than $10,000 in his personal bank account and owned no real estate, having embedded virtually all of his assets in his various companies. It would be Irving Broun, who had run the investment arm of the company, who would now serve as the president of the French Company, announced one month after French's death. Broun made it very clear at the outset that he would rely on the French Plan to further grow the company's real estate empire, a bit of news intended to let the financial community and general public know that despite nervous investors and the lingering economic crisis, it was business as usual.[174]

French's troubles with his famous financing plan and with his latest development, Knickerbocker Village, perhaps played contributing roles in his death, as each no doubt added considerable stress to his life. Built and launched during the heart of the Depression, Knickerbocker Village had turned out to be quite a different experience for French than Tudor City, which had benefited greatly from the economic boom of the late 1920s. With his new development draining money from his company in 1931, he had been forced to do the unthinkable. "French found it necessary, for the first time since the French plan had been inaugurated, to default on dividend payments on preferred stock in some of his projects," Rachlis and Marqusee wrote in their *The Land Lords*, with all holders of the stock understandably concerned.[175] Bank runs across the nation had begun in the fall of 1930, adding to the sense of panic among investors whose money was in the hands of large financial institutions.[176]

Of course, French was hardly alone having money problems in the world of real estate, as borrowing had become more difficult and more tenants were unable to pay their rents. Despite his attempts to silo his various companies and many buildings, the fact that they all fell into one very large pot could not be escaped. "French's pyramid of holding companies fell upon the usual hard times as the Depression developed," Alan Rabinowitz wrote in his informative *Urban Economics and Land Use in America*, "with rents received by the separate corporations falling to no more than one-half of 1920s peaks and with stock prices down to one-tenth of the price at which they had been issued." One might reasonably conclude that selling securities to develop large apartment buildings—the essence of the French Plan—was an excellent model when the economy was healthy but a terrible one when it was not.[177]

While some of these unhappy stockholders filed lawsuits against the French Company to try to recover some or all of the $14 million in dividends that were promised, Fred French had to deal with other legal troubles.[178] As part of Samuel Seabury's investigation of corruption within New York City government, it was revealed that French had paid $30,000 to the law firm of an ex–Tammany Hall official to ensure favorable decisions by the Board of Standards and Appeals regarding the height of the Fred F. French Building on Fifth Avenue and the zoning of Tudor City. "Various zoning changes were necessary if his plans were to be carried through to completion," Mackaye wrote in *The Tin Box Parade*, with a $75,000 bribe making that problem go away. French came before the Seabury committee in the fall of 1931, and while he admitted no wrongdoing, his reputation as the "Boy Wonder of Building" had been tarnished.[179] Still, there was no doubt at the time of his death that the man had made an important and lasting impact on New York City. French would be forever linked to some of the most important residential developments in the city—his legacy was ensured.

Thankfully, French had been able to witness the continued blossoming of Tudor City while dealing with more troubling matters. He had added four tennis courts to Tudor City in the spring of 1933, further contributing to the community's country club atmosphere. (The Tudor kings had played tennis, more justification to put in the courts.) True to form, French created valuable publicity around this latest amenity to attract tenants. In June of that year, he and his staff arranged for the tennis professionals Vincent Richards and Gil Hall to play an exhibition match to officially open the brand-new courts, with squash matches and handball and fencing events also part of the day's festivities.[180] Although Richards was a few years past his prime, landing him to help kick off the opening was newsworthy. As a fifteen-year-old, Richards had partnered with "Big" Bill Tilden to win the men's doubles at the U.S. National Championship in 1918, and six years later, he achieved a world ranking of no. 2.[181] A few years later, Tudor City's tennis courts had become the temporary home to a nationally recognized, professional tournament, quite a coup for the neighborhood. In July 1936, Joe Whalen beat Charles Wood to win that year's United States Pro Championship, the first and last time the event would take place on Tudor City's clay courts.[182]

As FDR finished his first term in 1936, it was clear that after some very tough years, the nation's economy was recovering. The infrastructure of New York City had changed much over the past few years, as millions of dollars of New Deal money poured into the building of new highways, bridges, parks, parkways, public housing and schools.[183] There were signs of new life at Tudor City as well. Twenty thousand tulip bulbs imported from Holland were planted in the private gardens in early 1936, the beginnings of what would be a long love affair between residents and the flower.[184] The forty-six varieties of tulips bloomed in the spring, a lovely way to celebrate the fact that before New York was New York, it was the Dutch colony New Amsterdam.[185]

Such events may seem trivial and corny today, but at the time they served as important ways to preserve the past and bring people together. The tulip show was also reflective of new efforts to make the city "green" and a greater recognition among both private and public officials of the importance of nature within the urban environment. Grass, plants and trees, for example, were currently being added to both sides of the East River (later FDR) Drive, which was initiated by the Works Project Administration and ran the seven miles between Grand Street and 125th Street. (The parkway was

Poster for "100 Water Colors" show held in Windsor Tower in 1940. Both creating and viewing art was a main activity at Tudor City between the world wars. *Wikimedia Commons.*

completed in 1942.) This landscaping, like the tulip show, was an indication of a heightened sensitivity to the natural world as the city further developed, an idea whose roots went back almost a century to the creation of Central Park and Brooklyn's Prospect Park.

Revisiting the first tulip show at Tudor City is indeed a trip through time. "Far from the land of windmills and dikes, an old Holland atmosphere descended upon Forty-second Street," a reporter captured the scene, with Borough of Manhattan president Samuel Levy providing the opening remarks. More than one thousand spectators watched children in colorful Dutch costumes perform folk dances, and a fashion show featuring floral patterns followed. Finally, prizes went to Tudor City residents who created the best paintings and took the best photographs of the gardens, further extending the show as a community-building event. The old-world theme was a perfect fit for the architectural motif of Tudor City and served as another prime example of French's talent for brand building. (This would be the only tulip show he would live to see.)[186]

A fair share of residents vying to win blue ribbons at that year's tulip show were no doubt members of the Tudor City Art Group. Various groups or clubs were formed at Tudor City, with tenants meeting regularly to share their particular interests. The Art Group was one such club, in which members discussed all things artistic and enjoyed outings to museums and galleries. One month after the tulip show, the group held a three-day Parisian street carnival at Tudor City, which re-created a portion of the old Latin Quarter of Paris. There were fortune-telling booths, puppet shows and hurdy-gurdys, injecting an odd slice of medieval French culture into a setting of early modern British architecture into a larger setting of twentieth-century New York City. Members of the group sketched drawings of visitors, while women wearing French peasant clothes sold balloons and a *gendarme* patrolled the grounds, adding to the carnivalesque atmosphere. Additionally, paintings, etchings, sculptures and other works by members were shown and sold, with all proceeds going to the club's fund to put on free exhibitions and lectures for the public. The event concluded with a masked ball in which some of the artists had created costumes, allowing those specializing in fashion to express their muse.[187]

The Center of Things

French's premature death would not allow him to see what were very good days for the neighborhood that he had created a decade earlier. With the economy rebounding nicely as the country began to prepare for possible war, the rental market in New York was robust, boding well for more upscale communities such as Tudor City. In September 1936, new and renewed leases at Tudor City were running 12 percent ahead of the previous year, the biggest jump in a single year since Black Monday (and allowing management to slightly raise the rents).[188] One year later, demand remained strong, additional evidence that the Great Depression was thankfully winding down.[189]

More good news was that the community's annual tulip festival was getting ever larger. Some fifty thousand flowers (courtesy of the Holland Bulb Growers Association) could be seen blooming in the park in the spring of 1937, more than twice the number the previous year when the festival debuted. Some three thousand people came to view the multicolored tulips, which included such varieties as the Darwin, Breeder, Orange Glow, John Ruskin, Argo, Goethe and Castor. The tulip display was now branded as "Holland Day in Manhattan," with Dutch-themed music and dance part of the event. A special part of the festival was *La Tulipe Noire*, a ballet that dramatized the development of the first black tulip in Holland in the seventeenth century. Government officials from the Netherlands were invited to be part of the occasion, with cash prizes and a trip to Holland awarded to the creator of the best artistic rendition of the garden.[190] With such prizes to be won, "the gardens were thronged with artists reproducing the scene in oils, watercolors and colored movies," a reporter noted the day after the festival.[191] There were eighty-eight submissions to that year's contest, which was judged by John Sloan, William Glackens and Walter Pach, all notable artists of the day (the former two were cofounders of the Ashcan School).[192] Some of the crowd visiting Tudor City for the first time no doubt came to the realization that the community would make a very nice place to live, exactly what the French Company intended in hosting the event.

The following year's tulip festival foreshadowed how Tudor City would in a few decades serve as an important site of activism and protest. Standing amid thirty thousand red, purple, white, orange and pink tulips, arranged in single-color beds, Nelson M. Wells, president of the City Gardens Club, voiced his concern about the city's air, which was in his words "seriously contaminated." Smoke and soot were indeed a problem in New York City at the time, with little or no regulation of automobile and factory noxious emissions. In fact, a group calling itself the Outdoor Cleanliness Association had been formed and chose the third annual Tudor City Tulip Festival to make its point. Plant life was damaged by sulfur dioxide in the city's air, Wells told the hundreds of flower enthusiasts who had gathered, challenging city officials to take action on the matter through legislation. Smoke also affected human beings, the organization added, anticipating the environmental movement of the 1970s.[193]

While flora was obviously welcome in Tudor City, fauna was less so, as the community reportedly became the first major apartment property in New York City to outlaw pet dogs. Landlords had always had to deal with residents' complaints about having a yappy dog as a neighbor, especially in high-rise buildings with many apartments. The war between dog owners and dogless tenants at Tudor City had escalated to the point where management decided to not lease apartments to those planning to bring their pet. Managers of the Marshall Field Garden Apartments in Chicago were taking more extreme action by telling all tenants of its 628 apartments that all dogs were no longer welcome there. Although dogs currently residing in Tudor City would not be evicted (and the community remained feline-friendly), canine-endowed tenants vigorously protested their landlord's anti-pooch stance.[194]

The French Company had bigger issues to deal with than trying to resolve squabbles between dog owners and light sleepers in the late 1930s. In early 1938, a group of stockholders of Woodstock Tower (formerly Tudor City Seventh Unit Inc.) formed a protective committee as a measure to oppose a reorganization plan put forward by French Company executive Aaron Rabinowitz. (In May 1937, Rabinowitz had been named a director and chairman of the board of the company's investing division, a post he would hold until his death in 1973.)[195] Holders of 6 percent preferred stock in the building would receive in exchange one share of "new prior" preferred, the plan proposed, with 345,000 shares of Class A common stock to be issued at the same time.[196] The financials were complicated, but it was clear that current stockholders did not like Rabinowitz's offer. More than three hundred of them met in February in what was described as a "lively meeting," with the reorganization plan flatly rejected.[197]

The good news for the French Company and most other real estate managers in Manhattan was that the economy was continuing to improve. The higher-end rental market was getting ever stronger in the city, as companies and the government added manager-level personnel and paid them generous salaries. War had broken out in Europe in September 1939 with Hitler's invasion of Poland, triggering an intensive military build-up in case the United States had to enter the conflict. "Beginning in mid-1940, when the federal government started to spend heavily on defense, industrial America emerged at long last from the Great Depression," wrote Williams.[198] Although Williams correctly noted that New York lagged behind other cities in terms of construction and manufacturing contracts and port activity, management fared far better than labor in terms of employment in 1940 and 1941. While blue-collar workers would have to wait until 1942 for their ship to come in, so to speak, white-collar employees were already reaping the benefits of the economic rebound. New York City was, of course, one of the country's corporate capitals, with probable war increasing the population of its managerial class along with money they had at their disposal.

This rejuvenation could easily be detected in Tudor City's 1940 advertising campaign. Not since the heady days of 1929 had the French Company been so jaunty and chirpy in promoting the community, with a much different story to now be told versus the desperate attempts to rent the place out in the early 1930s. The company returned to its once successful multi-target audience approach, with people in various life situations considered potential tenants. Housework-hating bachelors—a group that composed a large percentage of Tudor City residents in the Roaring Twenties—were again viewed as prime candidates, given the available maid, valet and laundry services and the three restaurants.[199] Families missing the action to be found in the city were another key target audience. Beyond the vast recreational, dining and shopping opportunities in Manhattan, bored and lonely suburbanites were again told, Tudor City itself offered a wide range of ways to socialize. With bridge, tennis and camera clubs as well as a dramatic group, Tudor City was an ideal place for those longing for a strong sense of community.[200]

Budget-conscious newlyweds were another market the French Company deemed worthwhile targeting in 1940. One-room apartments had fallen to as low as fifty dollars per month, making Tudor City stronger than ever in terms of the value it offered, the biggest bang for the buck.[201] But unlike the appeals made a decade earlier, Tudor City was also for those who did not have to watch their pennies. "They have the means to live where they please," copy of a May 1940 ad read under a photo of a well-dressed couple, "and they chose Tudor City because they like to be in the center of things."[202] Keeping die-hard New Yorkers in the city remained one of the company's "go-to" strategies; its managers knew that many young urban professionals were susceptible to being seduced by the bucolic suburbs. Couples not quite ready to settle down by having kids should stay in the city, one ad implied, lest they miss out on all the fun they could have while they still could.[203]

DOUBLING UP

The escalation of the war in Europe in 1941 could be detected at Tudor City in various ways. Even before the entry of the United States in the war, the community was showing support for the Allied forces. The spring tulip show took place as usual in 1941, but it was clear that there were bigger priorities. Obtaining fresh bulbs from Nazi-occupied Holland was understandably difficult at best, making this year's show tulip-less. (Ten thousand tulips were on display in the New York Botanical Gardens, but these were replants from bulbs that had been saved from 1939.) As in previous years, there was dancing, music and fashions, but in place of singing Dutch songs in the gardens, children from Tudor City's school, headed by Edna Traver, performed patriotic drills. Proceeds from the art exhibition went toward the British-American Ambulance Corps for the purchase of a four-stretcher, desert-type ambulance, another indication that things were quite different this year.[204]

Also different at Tudor City was that there were currently fewer tenants than in the late 1930s. Over the last few years, thousands of federal workers had left New York City for other American cities (notably Washington), part of the government's reallocation of resources in preparation for possible war. This was not good news for New York City landlords like the French Company, as empty apartments obviously meant less income. But beginning in the fall of 1941, the city was regaining some of these tenants as Uncle Sam opened up offices in Manhattan. Government agencies such as the Treasury Department and the Home Owners' Loan Corporation (which had been created by FDR in 1933 as part of the New Deal to help homeowners refinance their defaulted mortgages to prevent foreclosures) had recently set up shop in the city, for example, expanding the rental market. Some corporations that had moved New York–based personnel to defense plants scattered around the country were doing the same, this also helping to fill up some vacant apartments, including those at Tudor City.[205]

Of course, the easy walk to both the midtown business district and Grand Central Station was a good reason for some of these workers to choose Tudor City when apartment hunting. A walk through Grand Central today during rush hour would give some indication of how crowded that train station was day and night immediately before and during the war years. Of the country's nine ports, those shipping out were most likely to depart from New York City, with most soldiers and sailors arriving in the city by train before sailing. "Grand Central Terminal and Penn Station were jammed by GIs carrying duffel bags," Richard Goldstein observed in *Helluva Town*, his fine history of New York City during World War II. Those heading to points west could choose from the Twentieth Century Limited, which left Grand Central for Chicago every evening at 6:01 p.m., or the Broadway Limited, which departed from Penn Station.[206]

The prime location of Tudor City would become an even more important factor after the bombing of Pearl Harbor in December 1941 and the entry of the United States in the war. There were about four thousand residents spread out in eleven buildings and 2,800 apartments (in addition to the six-hundred-room hotel) in early 1942, with a good number of them involved in some aspect of the war effort. Most of the tenants worked in the midtown area, just as Fred French had anticipated, and many had lived in Tudor City for a decade or longer.[207] Space could still be had at Tudor City for new tenants, however, part of an active rental market that existed all the way from Greenwich Village to Washington Heights. (Although it would certainly be strange to do today, the *New York Times* regularly published the names, and sometimes even the occupations, of people who had signed rental leases, along with the respective addresses of the buildings they had chosen to live.)[208]

While the war raged in Europe and the Pacific during the summer of that year, those lucky enough to call Tudor City home enjoyed the various facilities in the community that remained in operation. Besides the two landscaped parks, the five clay tennis courts were often in use, especially among members of the Tudor City Tennis Club. Hundreds of feet higher, sunbathers sat in deck chairs, while others picnicked on top of the roofs of Prospect Tower, Tudor Tower and the Manor. The sundecks (which columnist Walter Winchell once dismissingly referred to as "Tar Beach") were especially popular on Saturdays and Sundays, and not simply because many did not work those days. It was not unusual for sewer gas fumes emanating from the Consolidated Gas Company located in Queens to drift across the East River, stinking up the East Side of Manhattan from downtown to midtown. To sunbathers' delight, the plant thankfully didn't operate on weekends.[209] A wading pool had been recently added to the community's playground area, complementing the slides, sandboxes and swings. More residents who would normally leave town for the summer were staying put because of the war and were finding city living during the warmer months to be more enjoyable than they had anticipated.[210]

Such pleasantries (and the fact that the buildings were fireproof and had steam heat) made Tudor City a highly desirable rental property through the early 1940s. Renewals were much higher than they had been in recent years, as vacant apartments across the city became increasingly scarce.[211] A new rental record was set in October 1942 when 740 leases were signed, not too surprising given the severe housing shortage during the war.[212] "The city's housing stock was in such short supply that more than 165,000 families were doubling up," according to Goldstein; the apartment-less were searching for anyone with an extra bedroom (or couch).[213]

The Metropolitan Scene

Not surprisingly, many army and navy officers were among the new tenants of Tudor City, part of the wartime "invasion" of New York City by military personnel and federal government workers. Tudor City was, in fact, attracting more than its fair share of sergeants, ensigns, lieutenants, captains and majors, again due to its convenient location and the ability to not pay for more space than one needed.[214] A good number of such tenants (11 percent, it was estimated by the French Companies) were moving out as soon as they got called to duty somewhere else, but still more (21 percent) were moving in, keeping the revolving doors in some of the buildings spinning.[215] The building, repairing and converting of ships that took place throughout the war at the Brooklyn Navy Yard was also bringing in thousands of people to the city. With some seventy-five thousand workers, the shipyard was by the end of the war the world's largest, helping to lay the foundation of the city's prosperity during the postwar era.[216]

As it had always done, the five-or-so-minute walk to Grand Central Station was definitely working in Tudor City's favor, as soldiers and sailors hopped trains to points elsewhere and then returned to their temporary home. With the wartime economy booming, businesspeople accounted for a fair share of new tenants. Other new renters were out-of-towners who, because of transportation limitations and fuel shortages in their area of the country, decided to move to Manhattan for the duration of the war emergency. Interestingly, a fair share of these out-of-towners were specifically choosing Tudor City because of its famous walkability, something they had enjoyed in their small towns. The high percentage of long-term residents was keeping Tudor City stable, however, a point of difference from smaller apartment buildings, where turnover was often much higher during the war. Tudor City was now 100 percent rented, with the waiting list to get in longer than ever. "Its renting experiences may be regarded as carrying wide significance in the metropolitan scene," beamed Broun, happy to report that Tudor City was more popular (and profitable) than it had ever been.[217]

One could easily see why fuel-short out-of-towners with the means were choosing New York City to sit out the war. Despite the government's urging to put all the extra cash one had into defense bonds, there was no shortage of ways to spend the money that had flooded into the city because of the war. Like everywhere else in homefront America, many goods were rationed and thus difficult to find, but a thriving black market in the city made it possible to get pretty much anything through a friend of a friend of a friend. One wouldn't know from the parties going on nightly in Manhattan that millions were dying in Europe, Asia and Africa. Department stores like Bonwit Teller and Saks were doing quite the business, and many Broadway shows were having no problem filling seats. Nightclubs like the Stork Club, El Morocco and the Copacabana were often packed, and many really were taking the A train to Harlem to see Duke Ellington and Count Basie at the Cotton Club. If that weren't enough, a new music called bebop could be heard on West 52nd (Swing) Street, and a new kind of art called abstract expressionism was seen at a gallery five blocks uptown.[218] It was not that long ago that thousands of New Yorkers stood in long breadlines and "Hoovervilles" sprang up in the city's parks, but the hard times of the Depression were now just a bad memory.

Even before the entry of the United States in the conflict, Tudor City residents, like many Americans across the country, were contributing to the war effort in myriad ways. Through 1940, a good number were donating clothing—suits, shoes, underwear and even old fur coats—to the Allied Relief Fund.[219] A few residents happened to be professional illustrators, cartoonists and artists, and these talented folks were asked to draw posters for the Red Cross.[220] Dozens of women were busy knitting sweaters, caps, socks and scarves and sewing dresses and baby clothes for Europeans whose countries had been invaded by the Nazis, with other residents donating money to buy the yarn. Dime jars were placed in the building lobbies for that purpose, and management set aside a workroom in the Woodstock Tower for the ladies to do their work.[221] Beginning in 1941, war bonds and stamps were sold at desks in all buildings under the auspices of the New York War Savings Staff (the "Minute Men" were also making the rounds with direct solicitations), with Tudor City tenants often winning the district's sales contest.[222]

As dozens of young men left Tudor City for military training in 1941, members of the local chapter of the American Women's Voluntary Services (AWVS) were keeping quite busy.[223] The AWVS, which included a fair number of Tudor City's society women, offered first-aid and other courses free to residents. (One, called "Fear and Morale," taught parents how to prepare their children for possible wartime emergencies.)[224] The AWVS held blood drives while community's Canteen Corps, also heavily female, fed soldiers on leave.[225] Other women were studying radio code, some of them receiving their FCC license, with yet others planning to enlist in the WAACs or WAVES.[226]

Management, meanwhile, with the help of the New York City police force, was offering tenants air raid instructions in case of a possible attack, which included turning off apartment lights, walking to designated locations and keeping away from windows.[227] Air raid wardens were appointed in each building, driven by concerns that New York City would, like London, be bombed or gassed. Should there be such an attack, go to the middle floors of your building, residents were told (the upper and lower ones were considered more dangerous), and take comfort in the fact that modern, steel-constructed structures like those of Tudor City were, relatively speaking, a good place to be.[228]

Still, Tudor City's building managers took seriously a potential wartime attack on New York City, with drills regularly conducted in which the "injured" were instructed to hide in different parts of the buildings and hopefully be found by air raid wardens.[229] Managers also worked with residents to set up first-aid stations in basements that were impressively equipped.[230] Despite New York City being considered a prime target for a possible enemy attack, rental queries poured into the offices of the French Company, many of them from Westchester County. Gas and tire rationing, as well as the fact that many domestics had joined up, were making suburbanites think the city would be a better place to spend the war. Many apartment complexes, including Tudor City, were benefiting from this influx in terms of occupancy rate.[231]

Privations could be also be found at Tudor City throughout the war, however, with little or no sugar to be found in the community's restaurants (under orders from the Office of Price Administration), and there was a limit of one cup of coffee per visit. A Salvage Committee at Tudor City urged residents to donate their scrap paper, rubber, fats and stockings, and the repainting and redecorating of apartments was put on hold (per the Office for Emergency Management).[232] In 1942, a pile of scrap metal stood in the spot where 42nd Street dead-ended at First Avenue, all of it collected from Tudor City residents discarding whatever they could for the cause.[233] Books, magazines, playing cards, records, games, radios and athletic equipment were collected for armed forces personnel, notably for those serving on merchant marine tankers that were equipped with rotating libraries.[234] In the spring of 1943, some residents even suggested that the two parks be dug up and converted to "Victory Gardens," in which homefronters grew vegetables as a food conservation measure, but thankfully the idea was rejected.[235]

A Tiny Parcel of Land

A casual observer might have that concluded that Christmastime in 1943 in New York City was much like any other, but a closer look would have indicated otherwise. Last-minute shoppers were hurrying about, and passersby were dropping coins and bills into Salvation Army kettles, making it hard to tell that a bitter world war was waging overseas. A tall tree, decorated with red-and-white globes and a shining star at the top, stood in Rockefeller Center, just as it had for the past decade. This year, however, there was one major difference. The tree was not illuminated, abiding by the government's instructions to save as much electricity as possible. Not lighting the tree was also in preparation of a blackout drill, which had begun taking place in the city the previous year. Mayor La Guardia ordered the drills, complete with air raid sirens, although many New Yorkers seemed to enjoy the rare chance to frolic in the city in almost total darkness.[236]

Those familiar with a traditional holiday event a few avenues and streets southeast also could detect that something seemed different this year. As usual on the night before Christmas Eve, four men dressed in Elizabethan garb carried a large oak log to one of the parks in Tudor City, where it was lit, with residents singing Christmas songs along with the Church of the Covenant choir while the Yule Log burned. The ritual had been a beloved part the community since 1934, save for 1942, when the event was cancelled because of the city's wartime lighting restrictions. The literally heartwarming scene was decidedly more melancholy this year, however, particularly for those whose loved ones were bravely serving their country.[237] Stalin, Roosevelt and Churchill had recently met in Tehran to try to coordinate efforts to defeat Germany once and for all, but in the meantime, the lives of millions of Americans remained in danger.

Happily, by the fall of the following year, it was becoming clear that the war would be ending relatively soon. Housing in New York City was expected to remain tight after the war as those in the war effort returned home (and, it would turn out, immediately start families). With Tudor City 100 percent rented, the French Company did not waste any time planning for its own future. In August 1944, the company announced that a new twelve-story building would be constructed after the war, providing 167 more apartments to the community. These apartments would have three or four rooms, making them significantly larger than the many single-room studios at Tudor City intended for one or two people but not as big as the five- and six-room suites at the Manor and Essex House. While the building would not be in the Tudor style, it would "harmonize" with its neighbors, the company made clear.[238]

Where would the French Company find space for what would become the first new building to be put up at Tudor City since 1930? During his wild buying spree in the late 1920s, French had attempted to acquire a four-story building on what the *New York Times* described as "a tiny parcel of land" that would help give him ownership of the entire area. French had planned to build the largest of his towers on the site, with the forty- or forty-five-story unit to be the flagship unit within Tudor City. As successful as he was in gobbling up parcels of land to add to his collection, French was unable to get the property due to one Joseph P. Zurla, who appeared to be as savvy as the esteemed developer. Zurla bought the plot in 1927 just as French was purchasing virtually everything that surrounded it, a smart move that the former clearly intended to use as leverage over the latter. After paying $27,000 for the property, Zurla reconfigured the four-story building to create seven small apartments that he rented out.[239]

French was determined to get one of the final pieces in his puzzle, however. In 1929, French offered $50,000, which Zurla promptly turned down. The bidding escalated to $185,000, but Zurla declined French's final offer, as he was reportedly holding out for $250,000. French cleared all the land surrounding the plot, a sign that he was willing to meet Zurla's demand, but as fate would have it, the market crash and subsequent Depression put a halt to most new construction projects. In another twist to the story, both French and Mr. Zurla died in 1936, with the war further shelving any new additions to Tudor City. But with the end of the war in sight in June 1945, the French Company and Zurla's estate were finally able to make a deal. The property was reportedly sold for a mere $40,000, awarding French a posthumous victory over his real estate rival.[240] It would be another decade for a new building to occupy that site, but somewhere Fred French may have been smiling, his position as the Boy Wonder of Building restored.

Chapter 3

THE CENTER OF THE WORLD, 1946–1959

Welcome neighbor.
–Warren C. Eberle, editor of the Tudor City View,
referring to the United Nations in January 1947

On November 17, 1946, Tudor City residents who had for many years taken the trolley along 42nd Street to go across town were in for quite a surprise. Rather than the trolleys that had been traversing that route since 1898, new diesel-powered buses were now running, a change that had already taken place on Third Avenue. Buses would replace the streetcars on Tenth Avenue that same day, as the city gradually modernized its mass transit system. The old trolleys would be sold at auction in a few days, likely headed to other countries, where they would remain in service for years to come. To celebrate the occasion, a luncheon was held at Tudor City, with Irving Broun, president of the Fred F. French Companies, presiding, and chairman of the city's Board of Transportation Charles P. Gross and Manhattan Borough president Hugo E. Rogers the honored guests. After lunch, Mrs. Charles Blakely, a resident of Tudor City, christened one of the buses "Miss Forty-second Street–Crosstown," which the guests promptly boarded on a maiden voyage to Times Square.[241]

Those who had been taking the trolley since William McKinley's first term as president and the sinking of the USS *Maine* may have been sad to see them go, but New York City as a whole was on the cusp of a major transformation. With the peace having been won, both the city and the nation were poised to embark on a new era of growth and prosperity that put behind the thrift and sacrifices made during the Depression and war years. The postwar years would prove to be a transitional period for Tudor City heavily defined by uncertainty and confusion, one that was sandwiched between the between-the-world-wars roller-coaster ride of prosperity and hard times and the turmoil and turbulence of the counterculture era. Residents of Tudor City would, completely unexpectedly, find themselves living a few blocks away from the "center of the world," something that proved to be a source of considerable friction and excitement. Much like the nation as a whole, Tudor City would experience anxiety and tension between the late '40s and early '60s, adding to the evidence that the postwar years were hardly a time of tranquility in America.

TUDOR CITY VIEW

Documenting the trajectory of Tudor City over the course of these years in elaborate detail was its house publication, the *Tudor City View*. Part solid journalism and part gossipy social calendar, the monthly *View* (which was distributed to each apartment at no cost) served as a seminal record of the goings-on of the community and, importantly, the lives of its residents. Births, deaths, marriages, engagements, illnesses, professional achievements and society happenings could be found in every issue. Stories with headlines like "Oldest Resident Dies," which reported the death of ninety-four-year-old Diana Huneker Lagen (the first woman sports editor on any American newspaper, whose cremated ashes were strewn from an airplane over the Atlantic Ocean), regularly appeared in the periodical, which was published between 1938 and 1969 (and as the *Tudor City Service* between 1934 and 1938, which was edited and published by W.L. Lightfoot).[242]

Much ado was made in *Tudor City View* of who was traveling where. Vacations as well as summer and winter plans were a mainstay of the publication. "Miss Jean Carmody, daughter of Mrs. Fifi Carmody of Windsor Tower, returned to Tudor City on August 25th, following a month's visit to Hollywood," readers learned in the September 1946 issue; the fact that "Miss Carmody made the trip both ways by air" was also considered newsworthy.[243] Gatherings of the community's tonier set made good copy. "Mr. and Mrs. Grancel Fitz entertained at a delightful cocktail party on Wednesday afternoon, September 18th, when fifty or more guests met on the roof garden of the Fitz's Windsor Tower studio apartment to greet Mr. and

Mrs. Jose Ferre, formerly of The Hermitage and now living in Ponce, Puerto Rico," envious residents found out the following month.[244]

Many residents believed that the French Company published *Tudor City View*, but this was not true. (The publication had a decidedly pro-company editorial slant, making it understandable why tenants thought so.) Warren C. Eberle, working out of an office in Windsor Tower, served as lead writer (with no byline), editor and publisher, with funding coming from advertising revenue. Eberle took over *Tudor City View* in January 1941 and put out 351 monthly issues until he (along with the publication) retired in May 1969, a remarkable achievement by any measure.[245] In addition to display and classified ads, there was a "Trading Post" section in each issue where residents could tell their neighbors what they wanted to sell or buy. A different photo of Tudor City was featured on each cover, adding an artistic element to the booklet or pamphlet-sized publication. Eberle's articles often were historical in nature, offering residents a deep understanding of the area and city in which they lived. Events at the Church of the Covenant on 42nd Street (often referred to as the "Church of Tudor City") were another staple that revealed the community's heavily Protestant (specifically Presbyterian) orientation.

Tudor City View clearly reflected the small-town nature of the community that Fred French believed would appeal to urbanites considering fleeing the often impersonal city. "Miss Esther Waine, who has charge of the 'Lost and

Church of the Covenant, the unofficial church of Tudor City. *Photo by Piero Ribelli.*

Found Department' of Tudor City, has several pairs of gloves, a pair of spectacles, and a coin purse which no one has claimed," read a July 1948 item.[246] The gentle chastising of residents for a variety of offenses was a regular feature, something unlikely to be found in a big-city paper. Tenants were warned to not put flower pots or electric irons on windowsills, lest a gust of wind make them fall on an unwary pedestrian, and the shaking of dust mops out windows was another no-no. Lit cigarettes were also being thrown out of windows, sometimes landing in a neighbor's apartment one floor below, and a rash of fires prompted Eberle to urge residents to not smoke while lying down. Scantily clad sunbathers in the parks was a less serious problem but one that seemed to irk Eberle given how often he brought it up. Tenants were also advised to curb their dogs and turn off the lights when leaving their apartments to save the landlord money. (Then, as now, electricity was included in the rent.)

More than anything else, however, *Tudor City View* illustrated how social the community was, especially during the postwar years. Club activities, in which members got together to share a common interest, were regularly featured. The Camera Club was particularly active, with amateurs sharing their photos and invited professionals giving talks and tips. "Lt. Gae Faillace of Hotel Tudor will display colored movies and Kodachrome stills taken by him during the war against Japan, in the Windsor Tower, Grey Room, on Thursday, evening, September 19th," went a typical item from 1946, with bus trips to scenic locales like farms and state parks organized as opportunities for members to take photos.[247] The Tudor City Forum, in which one to a dozen people got together on the first and third Tuesdays of every month, was another enthusiastic group. Forum members held "friendly discussion of topics of current importance" on a round-robin basis, with no politics allowed. (In January 1947, the talks were "The Basis of a Sound Labor Policy and an Equitable Industrial Relationship" and "How Should Family Finances Be Handled?")[248] "Since the group is small, everyone is given an opportunity for self-expression and no one is permitted to monopolize the discussion," readers of *Tudor City View* who were considering attending a meeting were assured.[249]

Beyond such specific-interest clubs, there was a general Tudor City Club located in Woodstock Tower, in which residents gathered to play bridge, gin rummy, backgammon, chess, checkers and canasta or just read magazines.[250] The club was open every evening except Sunday and charged no dues. Some form of entertainment could also often be had in the club, as the occasional evening when the Manor resident and professional hypnotist David Tracy put on an exhibition. "The most amusing stunt of the evening was that in which six subjects accepted and simultaneously carried out six different suggestions," it was reported in November 1946, with Tracy hopefully snapping participants out of it before the meeting was adjourned.[251]

It's hard to estimate the value of such a club in these days before television and, much later, web surfing and social media took up much of our leisure time. A letter sent in December 1946 by sixty-two residents and friends of Tudor City to Charles N. Blakely, an executive at the French Company, revealed how important the club was to them:

> *We who are not native New Yorkers find the Club an ideal rendezvous for our social activities; and we particularly cherish the Club because we had been led to believe that New York is a cold and avaricious city. Fortunately for Tudor City residents and their friends, however, a true community spirit has been born of the pleasant associations and neighborliness of our club. We feel a new loyalty to this small segment of teeming New York, finding here the desirable quantities of suburban life at the very portals of the world's largest city.*[252]

Terra Incognita

The conversion of the streetcars to buses on the East Side in the late 1940s served as a prime example of the postwar march to progress that, at the same time, seemed to carry a certain cost. "Take a good look at the Forty-Second Street Crosstown [street]cars, whose pokiness you have probably cursed time and again," *Tudor City View* editor and publisher Warren Eberle advised his readers, happy to report that they would soon "give way to buses, and let us hope, to speedier crosstown service."[253] In less than a year, however, he appeared less than convinced that the diesel buses, which were now replacing the streetcars on Third Avenue, represented a sign of progress. "We shall miss those conveyances which didn't throw us off our feet every time they started and which could be counted on to stop somewhere near street intersections instead of sailing by their proper stopping places, leaving us stranded, because they happened to open their doors fifty or seventy-five feet down from the corner," he wrote in March 1947 after a few crosstown experiences. And while those new buses would be, like the ones on the 42nd Street route, faster and cleaner than the trolleys, Eberle doubted that "their drivers will hardly be as courteous or as polite as the old men who have been sitting at the [street] car controls."[254]

Conveniently, the retiring of Manhattan's trolleys coincided with the twenty-first "birthday" of Tudor City, a good reason to take a look back on the formation of what was now a thriving community on Prospect Hill. Fred French's 1925 announcement that he would build a large high-rise apartment complex in the down-and-out area took many by surprise, but his vision had been largely achieved. About 5,500 residents were now living in the community's 2,800 apartments, fewer than the population of 10,000 in the city-within-the-city that he had imagined, but there remained room for growth.[255] With some machinations, it would be possible to squeeze more buildings into the area, something that the current management was pondering. And with the eight acres of meatpacker property along the East River being finally acquired (brokered by already legendary real estate mogul William Zeckendorf of the firm Webb and Knapp), rumors began circulating that another major building project that would adjoin Tudor City was in the works.[256] Whatever rose on the site, tenants of Tudor City were delighted to see the slaughterhouses, stockyards, coal yards and other unattractive elements go. "It will not be long now until the First Avenue abattoirs, which have had a disconcerting habit occasionally of making their proximity too obvious, will soon be a matter of history to be written up by those of us who like to reminisce on the by-gone days of New York," it was noted in *Tudor City View* in October 1946.[257]

While the future of Tudor City was, of course, uncertain, all would agree that the development had in its first twenty-one years become a recognized neighborhood of New York City. Tudor City was "one of the first projects of its type in Manhattan, and still ranks as one of the biggest residential groups anywhere," the *New York Times* reported, quite an accolade for something created essentially from scratch. And just as French promised, ownership of the property remained with the original stockholders, and the value of the securities of the buildings had significantly increased, good news for all parties.[258]

Very soon, however, it was becoming increasingly clear that rather than another Tudor City–like development, it would be the United Nations (UN) that would soon occupy the slaughterhouse site. The UN had set up shop in Lake Success on Long Island as temporary quarters while waiting for a permanent home to be established. The organization was considering Philadelphia, of all places, as its new home, something that devout New Yorkers like William Zeckendorf found unacceptable. Zeckendorf quickly (eight days, in fact) brokered a deal with the Rockefeller family to buy the property for $8.5 million (about $100 million today) and then donate it to the

UN. "Though some, particularly supporters of competing cities, objected that the decision was made too hastily, the generosity of John D. Rockefeller Jr. was applauded widely throughout the world," Pamela Hanlon wrote in her 2017 *A Worldly Affair*, with what would soon be called the "center of the world" to be located a football field or two away from Tudor City.[259]

Once this exciting news got out, the media turned its attention turned to the less than impressive site. "Our scout has returned from a tour of inspection

View of United Nations Plaza from Tudor City, circa 1966. *Library of Congress, Prints and Photographs Division.*

of the seventeen acres, more or less, which lie along the East River between Tudor City and Beekman Place," a *New York Times* reporter wrote two days before Christmas 1946, with the tour revealing that the area between the two popular residential communities was "terra incognita." Some cattle pens could still be seen in what the reporter considered "the dingiest and most neglected part of the sunrise side of Manhattan," and the "raw material of beefsteaks, roasts, and chops" could clearly be seen from First Avenue.[260]

It would not be long, however, for the cows of midtown Manhattan to be relocated to literally greener pastures. While the news about the UN's impending arrival likely made most New Yorkers proud, residents of Tudor City recognized that they would have a special relationship with the organization being next-door neighbors. In January 1947, Eberle nicely articulated this awareness of having some kind of extra stake in the matter:

> *The world's political center is to be located but a stone's throw from us, across First Avenue. We cannot help feeling a sense of importance on this account* [as we have a] *role to play in the continuance and strengthening of good international relationships, for some of the secretariat are likely to find homes in Tudor City. We shall have an opportunity to prove how sincerely we are concerned with international peace and amity, by the spirit of tolerance with which we accept these representatives of other nations and hail them as fellow citizens of the "One World"—at least in spirit and aspiration for a secure and peaceful social order.*[261]

In that same issue of *Tudor City View*, French Company chairman Aaron Rabinowitz offered his thoughts on the exciting news. He, too, recognized that it could be the beginning of a beautiful friendship between the UN and Tudor City:

> *New Yorkers may well be proud that their city has been selected as the permanent home site of the United Nations. And we of Tudor City rejoice in the promised transformation which is to give our immediate neighborhood a group of splendid buildings in place of the unsightly and unsavory structures of today. But best of all from our vantage point is the added dignity which Tudor City will acquire and the pride with which its residents can boast of living next door to the international capital where leaders of every nation will be working for the creation of a better world.*[262]

Grandstand Seats

With the wheels set in motion and the backing of Rockefeller money, the City Planning Commission moved quickly to impose new zoning restrictions in the area. Heading up the project was city construction coordinator Robert Moses, who for the past few decades had become known for his building projects that prioritized automobile mobility over everything else. It was unclear how large of an area these restrictions would cover, but the French Company was concerned, as it owned land one block west of Tudor City that it planned to develop with apartment buildings. Height restrictions on buildings would reduce the possible number of stories and apartments, meaning of course less potential rental income.[263] In May 1947, the zoning restrictions were approved by the Board of Estimate, putting in place a range of rules affecting Tudor City's larger neighborhood of east midtown Manhattan. No new breweries, crematories, blacksmith shops, public garages and dance halls could be constructed in the area, as all of these businesses presumably were deemed by the City Planning Commission as potentially offensive to the world leaders who would be working at the United Nations. Height restrictions on new construction were also approved—bad news for the French Company, which was planning to put up at least one more tall building on vacant property that adjoined Tudor City.[264]

While such a building would no doubt be easily rented given the acute housing shortage in the city, finding the funds to construct it was currently not possible. The French Plan was no longer an option given investors' memory of what had happened during the Depression, and financial institutions were reluctant to give developers loans because of the current real estate climate. The federal government had frozen rentals since March 1, 1943, as a means to protect wartime and postwar tenants from price gauging. Inflation and expenses had gone up, however, leaving landlords like the French Company between a rock and a hard place. With inadequate income and money tight, most developers could not put up new buildings even though current ones, including Tudor City, were 100 percent rented. Public housing for families with low incomes was popping up across the city, but the members of the middle class had little opportunity to find apartments that fit their needs and budget. The real estate industry was asking Congress to allow increases, but so far, no action had been taken.[265]

Fully aware that many Tudor City residents were finding their one-room apartments to be claustrophobic and were on a waiting list for bigger ones should they come available, French Company president Irving Broun decided to appeal directly to them to see things from his perspective. "We firmly believe that a fair rent increase is both necessary and advisable not only in justice to thousands of people who are directly or indirectly interested in the ownership of residential rental property, but in the best interests of the general public as well," he wrote in an "Open Letter to All Tenants" published in *Tudor City View* in May 1947, "particularly those families who are now finding it so difficult to obtain suitable housing accommodations."[266] Well into the 1950s, the French Company and many other landlords in the city continued to push for rental increases, frustrated by laws in place inhibiting the supply and demand of the market.[267]

Meanwhile, the redevelopment of the area along Manhattan's East River continued to march ahead. By September of that year, demolition of the stockyards and slaughterhouses had begun, with reports that even the notorious odor of the packinghouses had disappeared. For residents of Tudor City, a tall structure would in a few years be blocking a good chunk of the view of the river (the UN building was completed in 1952 at a cost of $68 million), but no longer would they have to endure the smell of cattle processing when the wind was drifting southwest.[268] A few months later, the city, at the French Company's request, approved a new name for Prospect Place: Tudor City Place. Some mail had been going to Brooklyn's (larger) Prospect Place and other mail to the similarly named street in the Bronx. Taxicabs also occasionally took passengers to Brooklyn when hearing them say "Prospect Place," another reason for the name change.[269]

Through the early months of 1948, those living along sweet-smelling Tudor City Place pondered how the development of the UN might affect their community. It was impossible to know that its addition to the east midtown neighborhood of Manhattan would alter the very identity and chemistry of Tudor City and propel it into a new and more complicated orbit. Fifty buildings in the slaughterhouse and stockyard district were being demolished for the UN project (one was left standing for workers to occupy), and 270 residents of nearby tenements were either relocated or compensated in cash. A world-class team of architects, including Frenchman Le Corbusier and Russian Nikolai Bassov, was hired to collaborate on the project, with all signs indicating that something truly amazing would rise on the site.[270] "One thing is certain," Eberle wrote, thinking that "for the next four or five years, Tudor City residents are destined to occupy grandstand seats overlooking one of the most stupendous and interesting construction jobs that man has tackled since the beginning of time."[271]

A PRIVILEGED POSITION

Not only would Tudor City residents be able to watch the construction job from grandstand seats, but they also would soon find themselves in the game itself. Mayor O'Dwyer had put Moses fully in charge of the UN project, and the man whose greatest expertise was arguably building bridges and tunnels for automobiles believed that traffic control should be the priority in the redevelopment plan. A wider 42nd Street would not only ease traffic around the site but also serve as an impressive approach to the UN, Moses reckoned, thinking that about $15 million (about $153 million today) would get the job done.[272] Soon, however, it became clear that the mammoth project would encroach on the little village that had sprung up two decades earlier. The city intended to widen Tudor City Place as part of its master plan for the development of the broader UN area, French Company and residents learned during the summer of 1948, the news being completely consistent with Robert Moses's modus operandi.[273]

It was unclear exactly how the widening of the cul-de-sac street would be helpful to the comings and goings of vehicles related to the construction and operations of the UN down below on First Avenue, but with Moses in charge, it was essentially a done deal. There was only one way to get the strip of land needed to widen Tudor City Place that ran directly through the community: the two private parks would have to be narrowed, something considered anathema by virtually all tenants and illegal by the French Company. The bad news was duly noted in the *Tudor City View*. "Tudor City Place is not an approach to the United Nations' site and has no connection (except for a stairway) with any approach thereto," Eberle argued in July 1948, asking, "By what stretch of imagination can such a change be of the remotest value to the UN project?" Moses would get his wider street by removing the Litch Gates, the arbors and much of the shrubbery, plus some of the seating space in South Park and play space in North Park, it was revealed, a real shock to Tudor City residents, who cherished their green space.[274]

The French Company also was not happy to hear that the city intended to appropriate some of its private parkland and quickly circulated a petition among the residents to fight back. Tudor City Place didn't even directly link with the UN site, the petition correctly pointed out, and widening the private street would make the crossing of it by residents more hazardous by increasing vehicular traffic.[275] As many as 2,678 residents signed the petition, which was presented a few weeks later to Mayor William O'Dwyer; the local media took notice of the latest battle between Robert Moses and concerned citizens. (The story made front-page news in the *New York Herald Tribune*.) But with the city's "power broker" in charge, it appeared that Moses was, as usual, going to have his way. "Tudor City has enjoyed a privileged position up there for a long time," senior engineer of the Borough of Manhattan Harry W. Levy commented; the fact that the park was private and that taxes had always been paid on it made little difference.[276] "Sorry boys, but Bob Moses wants it that way and nothing can be done about it," Mayor O'Dwyer remarked after French Company executives protested the land grab, with even the city's top elected official knowing that Moses had the ultimate say in what was constructed and what wasn't.[277]

This was the beginning of what would turn out to be a decades-long war for residents to protect and preserve their precious parks. This battle would be lost, however. "We're licked," Eberle sadly wrote in September as it became clear that the city was legally permitted to claim private property as it saw fit. Two months later, the Board of Estimate voted to acquire title to the designated property along Tudor City Place, the explanation being that the greater width was necessary to build a bigger street crossing over 42nd Street. (Another reason given was that more space was needed for all the visitors who would soon be looking down on the construction project as it progressed, with yet another asserting that the street was currently too narrow to turn fire engines around.) Whatever the justification, the two parks would be narrowed by twenty-two feet, a not insignificant amount given their relatively small size.[278] While residents would mourn the loss of some of their private paradise, Eberle tried to look on the bright side as ground was broken in September 1948. "The period of reconstruction will result in inconveniences [but] if the United Nations can make a contribution to the cause of world peace, that inconvenience will be worthwhile," he reasoned that same month.[279]

Some residents, however, were convinced that the rise of the UN would result in much more than some manageable inconveniences. Rumors were circulating that Tudor City would soon be or already had been purchased, although it was not clear by whom. One story had it that the Duke of Windsor was buying the community, another that the investment firm Lehman Brothers had already purchased it. But the most popular rumor was that the United Nations Organization itself was trying to buy the community from the French Company in order to house its thousands of personnel. (Housing for the UN workers was initially planned but never built.)[280] The company tried to allay such fears, but the concern that all residents would soon be evicted to make room for the UN people persisted.[281] A more reasonable story making the rounds was that just the Woodstock Tower on 42nd Street would be appropriated by the city for the UN, with the French Company again having to explain that tenants in that building need not fret.[282]

Eberle used his platform to try to dispel Tudor City residents' suspicion that they had better start looking for a new place to live. "If real estate brokers could collect commissions on all the rumored sales of Tudor City, they could spend the next year at Miami or Waikiki Beach, with never a worry about expenses," he wrote in February 1949, plainly stating that "tenants may calm their fears."[283] Many Tudor City residents were among the crowd of sixteen thousand watching President Truman lay the cornerstone of the Secretariat Building on October 24, 1949, some of them no doubt still wondering if UN workers would soon be occupying their apartments.[284] Soon, however, a counter-rumor was circulating that the French Company was happy to see the UN rising in hopes that, given the current state of world affairs, it would fail and its new headquarters would be put up for sale. With the clamor for more and bigger apartments, a very large and vacant UN building would be a valuable addition to Tudor City, this contingent argued, seeing the glass as half full versus half empty.[285]

A NUMBER OF HEADACHES

Given the contentious goings-on at the UN's temporary digs at Lake Success at midcentury, perhaps those dreaming of an apartment with significantly more square footage in a brand-new modern building would get their wish. "The U.N. has become little better than a noisy debating society," Eberle opined in October 1950, with Cold War tensions crushing the hopes of international harmony at the end of World War II.[286] Meanwhile, Tudor City residents vigorously debated the architectural merits of the 550-foot-tall Secretariat Building after seeing the renderings. Some believed that the glass and marble building looked like a giant tombstone, and they were disappointed to see that it belonged to no recognizable architectural school or genre. Others found the openness and lightness of the structure refreshing and delighted in the possibility that some of its more than five thousand windows would reflect onto Tudor City, hopefully as the sun set in the west over the Hudson. For still others, the sheer solidity of the enormous rectangle offered a much welcome sense of security in these dangerous times, affording some confidence that there would be a world to wake up to each morning.[287] The Secretariat Building received mixed reviews from the professional architect community as well, with some of the most famous architects of the day—including Frank Lloyd Wright, Philip Johnson and Lewis Mumford—equally divided on its aesthetics.[288]

Indeed, just like citizens in many communities across the country during the Cold War, Tudor City residents feared that a nuclear war with the Soviet Union was a distinct possibility and actively prepared for such. (Manhattan, especially the east midtown area, was considered a prime target for possible attack given the proximity of Grand Central Station, rising United Nations, large media companies and utility plants along and tunnels through the East River.) Concerned that Tudor City was in a significant danger zone, tenants in each building regularly held civil defense meetings, and air raid wardens were appointed to lead bomb drills. The palpable anxiety recalled the times during World War II, when an attack by German subs off the coast or planes from above was considered a real threat.

Tudor City residents also had to live with the fact that for the next few years, a construction project of major proportions would be taking place literally in their backyard. The city's recent land grab also made it clear that this wasn't your run-of-the-mill project, but rather one that involved local, state, federal and even international officials, some of whom held considerable political power. As in 1942 because of the wartime blackout, there was no Yule Log ceremony during Christmastime of 1950 due to the UN work, a good example of the "inconveniences" that tenants would have to endure for at least the next few years.[289] "With this work in prospect, one's mood is much like that of the person who must live in a home during alterations or stay in an apartment while it is bring painted," Eberle grumbled in January 1951; like most residents, he was already weary of how the new neighbor had disrupted their previously peaceful community.[290] "There is general agreement that one year of stumbling over uneven sidewalks, dodging traffic on the detour and 'making-do' with the disheveled sections of our park is sufficient suffering to be borne for the improvements that are to follow," he groused a year later.[291]

Unfortunately, considerably more suffering was in the cards, as the city was hardly done altering the Tudor City neighborhood to facilitate the development of the UN campus. (The Secretariat Building, Conference Building and General Assembly Building were formally completed in October 1952.)[292] The lowering of 42nd Street seventeen feet directly in front of Woodstock Tower as part of the "improvement" plan for the UN had required the owners of the building—French Plan shareholders—to drop its lobby by a full floor. Some useable space had also been lost in the building, according to the attorneys, justification to add this to the growing tab they would submit to the city's financial manager.[293] It wasn't just stockholders (and residents) of Woodstock

Tower who were unhappy about what the city was doing to literally pave the way for the UN, ostensibly to relieve potential traffic jams in the area. The entrances to three other buildings located on that stretch of 42nd Street—the Tudor Hotel, the Hospital for Special Surgery (which would be taken over by Beth David Hospital in a few years) and the Church of the Covenant—were now well above street level, forcing them to also have to figure out a way for people to get in and out. (Attendance at the church's services had dropped along with 42nd Street, with the pastor understandably upset that not only would a new entrance have to be built but that about $50,000 in contributions had also been lost because of the construction work taking place in front.) The regrading of 42nd Street had also made it impossible for anyone to get to or go from Tudor City by car except via 41st Street, and reaching 42nd Street by foot was now possible only by walking down a steep stone stairway that had been recently built. "The change of grade, while a boon to the United Nations, has caused a number of headaches for a number of Tudor City residents," the *New York Times* noted in March 1952, the worse news being that the project was running behind schedule.[294]

Woodstock Tower stockholders sought more than a few aspirins to get rid of the headache they endured by having to drop their building's lobby a floor. Lawyers acting in the interests of their client demanded that the city pay $1 million (subsequently reduced to $826,709) as compensation for the necessary alterations to the building and for the loss of hundreds of thousands of dollars in rental income because of the city's construction work.[295] While the Woodstock Tower shareholders would not get their $826,709, they were soon awarded $405,000 for the necessary changes resulting from the regrading. The apartment building had, in fact, not lost any rental income over the past year, the city's bean counters had discovered, the reason why $400,000 of its claim was dismissed.[296] The Tudor City Hotel received $100,535 of the $165,352 it had asked the city for, while the Church of the Covenant was awarded $90,000 on its claim of $250,000.[297]

There were other good reasons why Tudor City residents and the French Company experienced a number of headaches between the late 1940s and early 1950s. Showers of soot from the Consolidated Edison Company plant at 14th Street and East River continued to be a pervasive problem for many, as the residue of burning coal poured into apartments and permeated clothing, rugs and drapes.[298] Smoke stacks reaching hundreds of feet in the air were added to the Con Ed plant at First Avenue and 40th–41st Streets, where electricity was generated from coal, but this appeared to do little to solve the problem of soot coming from this facility that was right around the corner from Tudor City.[299] Nearly a ton and half of soot per city block fell from the sky each month, it was estimated, five times the amount that had rained down in 1941. It wasn't just utility companies like Con Ed (which owned the six blocks east of First Avenue between 35th and 41st Streets) that were responsible for the dispersion of the black ash; steamer ships, chimneys, freight trains and building incinerators were also major contributors. Pittsburgh and St. Louis each had a similar problem some years back, but ways were found to eliminate much of those industrial cities' soot production, suggesting that it could be done in New York City as well. An organization called the Committee for Smoke Control was pushing city officials hard to pass more stringent measures regulating the amount of soot that could be released, but this was little consolation to residents spending considerable time trying to keep their apartments, furnishings and clothing clean.[300]

The French Company certainly didn't need the negative publicity it received and fully deserved after it was revealed that Tudor City continued to enforce racist policies after the war, at least unofficially. In 1948, Claude Marchant, an African American, had been awarded $1,000 by a city court jury as compensation for being denied use of a passenger elevator at Tudor Tower on two separate occasions. The twenty-four-year-old dance instructor was visiting a friend who lived in the building and was forced to use a service elevator (which was used for moving garbage). While the federal Civil Rights Act of 1964 was sixteen years away, New York had already passed a State Civil Rights Law, making the exclusion illegal. The French Company denied the allegation, said that no discrimination had taken place and planned to make an appeal. Meanwhile, the jury's decision would be "hailed by minorities everywhere as a victory for liberty and justice and a defeat for intolerance," Mr. Marchant declared after leaving the court. The incident was a small one but presaged the civil rights movement looming ahead.[301]

A FIERCE AND RUTHLESS BREED

Fortunately, by the fall of 1952, it had become clear that the city's improvement plan for the UN was close to being finished, and all would agree that what had been built was vastly superior to the slaughterhouses that had occupied the site for a half century or so. "The towering green-windowed structure that houses the Secretariat and the General Assembly Hall just north of it make an imposing group," observed Meyer Berger for the *Times* in October, thinking that the redevelopment of the area "would startle any urban Rip

Van Winkle who might come upon it without warning."[302] Over the next year, the UN would become the most popular tourist destination in the city, as word of mouth spread across the country and around the world about this amazing new building in which the people inside were doing what they could to further international understanding. The establishment of the UN also did much to reaffirm the relevancy of New York City at a time when many people and companies were fleeing to the suburbs. Some big corporations had recently relocated from Manhattan to Westchester, notably White Plains, but the presence of the UN served as more evidence that Gotham remained the cultural, political and economic capital of the world in the 1950s.[303]

On an equally happy note, Fred French's vision of a larger "city within a city" was on the way to becoming a reality. The groundbreaking in March 1954 for a new fifteen-story building with 334 "modern" apartments was viewed as very good news, as the expansion of the community was proof positive that it remained alive and well. A quarter century had gone by since the last building in Tudor City had been erected, with the number of apartments frozen at 2,800 plus the 500 rooms at the Tudor Hotel. This building, which would be called the Tudor Garden Apartments, was being referred as a "multi-family structure," a smart move given the number of baby boomers being born and raised in the 1950s. The two-wing, U-shaped structure (with an underground garage) would have apartments from two to five and a half rooms, much bigger than the studios in the earlier buildings, and rent between $140 and $359 per month. For the first time, the French Company was partnering with another real estate developer (Gandolfo Schimenti, which had built a good number of high schools in the city) to foot the $5 million construction bill, with no apparent plans to sell securities in the building to the public as under the "French Plan."[304]

Tudor City Gardens would sit on the fifty-five-thousand-square-foot plot that had previously served as the site of the community's prized tennis courts. With court rental just $1 to $3 per hour, depending on day and time, playing tennis at Tudor City after the war had understandably been a popular pastime since they had been added to the community in 1933.[305] Some played just for fun, but others were determined to climb the ladder of rankings that were kept or do well in the annual tournament (divided into Class A and B singles and doubles).[306] Famous people could sometimes be spotted on the courts, attracting the paparazzi of the day. Katharine Hepburn, who lived nearby in Turtle Bay Gardens, had taken lessons from Elwood Cooke, who ran the facility for many years, and professionals sometimes hit balls there. Bobby Riggs, Jack Kramer, Pancho Gonzales, Frank Parker and Pancho Segura played there in 1949 to prep for their professional matches to be held in Madison Square Garden.[307] A United Nations Club had been formed after the war, with exhibition matches played annually on courts. (Bobby Riggs played Elwood Cooke in the 1951 exhibition.)[308] In 1947, the owner of a chain of parking lots had offered the French Company $15,000 per year to rent the site—several times more than what the company was making from court time fees. The company declined, however, thinking that a parking lot would detract from the quality of life in the community (and likely knowing that it would need that land when it was ready to put up a new building).[309]

With developing rental properties difficult at best after the war because of capital constraints, it wasn't until 1954 that the French Company was able to use the site of the tennis courts for what would become Tudor City Gardens. While the building would not be designed in the Tudor style, the architect, William I. Hohauser (one-time employer of his more famous cousin, Henry Hohauser), used red brick to at least complement the other buildings. The crescent-shaped covered entrance and glass-enclosed lobby with terrazzo floors was pure postwar aesthetic, however, making it obvious that the building was a product of a different era. Maid, valet and laundry services were available, however, a throwback to the host of amenities offered between the wars. Just as the Tudor City buildings of the late 1920s and early

The decidedly postwar 2 Tudor City Place, which was built on the site of the much-enjoyed tennis courts. *Photo by Piero Ribelli.*

1930s were as modern as could be on the inside, so would this building take advantage of all the latest home technology of its day, including cavity walls (for better insulation), fluorescent lighting and, in the larger units, automatic dishwashers. Free connection with a "Master Television Aerial" would also be available to tenants, this technology offering significantly better reception than the "rabbit ears" that often had to be almost continually adjusted to get a decent picture.[310] (Television reception had always varied dramatically by building and location of apartment in the community, with residents known to rearrange their furniture in order to locate the set where it most often worked best.)[311] Tudor City Gardens would be the last building to be part of Tudor City, however, as there simply wasn't any more room to put up another.[312]

While many Tudor City residents who wanted to stay in the community but longed for a larger apartment were happy to see the new building go up, others were disappointed to learn that the tennis courts were no more. Besides those who played the sport, residents whose apartments were on the lower floors of Windsor Tower would no longer be able to see the sunsets behind Empire State Building, an occupational hazard of living in an ever-changing, ever-rising city. The French Company no doubt celebrated its arrival, and not just because it would have an additional revenue stream alongside its other rent-controlled buildings. The new building was a quarter century late in coming—not as big as the mammoth, fifty-four-story building that Fred French had planned for that space in the late 1920s that had been quashed by the Depression, but a sizable property nonetheless. (That building would have contained more apartments than all the others in Tudor City combined, as well as a swimming pool and auditorium.) The twelve-story building planned to be put up soon after the war had also not come to be because of economics, making the realization of Tudor City Gardens a sweet victory for the fair number of French Company executives who had worked there for decades.[313]

Perhaps in part because of the new status the United Nations had brought to midtown east Manhattan, Tudor City's newest and final building was proving to be a hit as it was rented out. The severe housing shortage had continued after the war, something Dan Wakefield noted in his memoir of the decade, *New York in the 50s*. In 1956, Wakefield moved to Greenwich Village to immerse himself in the bohemianism, bebop and beat culture to be found in that part of town, but finding an affordable apartment was hardly easy despite rent control. "Reasonable rents (forget about cheap) were still possible but damnably scarce," he recalled, with apartment hunters "a fierce and ruthless breed," waiting at newsstands for the first copies of the

Voice and the *Villager* to try to get a jump on the others. Spending the night on line at a newsstand awaiting the arrival of the *New York Times* was also not unusual at the time, after which one had to "dash to a phone to try to make a deal or be on the doorsteps of realtors or landlords at dawn" if one hoped to snag an apartment.[314]

Wakefield would not have been caught dead in the suburbs, but the housing shortage was impetus for less hip residents of the city to look there for a place to live. Many had in fact done so, but by the mid-'50s, there were signs that the migration was reversing. For whatever reasons, Tudor City Gardens was becoming a popular destination for suburbanites who were apparently following Fred French's prescription to be able to walk to work and enjoy all that Manhattan had to offer. In June 1955, the local NBC television station interviewed a couple from Westport, Connecticut, who had just signed a lease there, with viewers hearing how delighted they were to be back in the thick of things.[315]

Tudor City was again in the televisual news just a few months later when CBS newsman Ed Murrow decided to drop in on Charlton Heston and his family at the actor's fabulous Windsor Tower penthouse apartment (Studio 7). While giving the appearance of a friendly social call, the interview was actually a carefully orchestrated piece of publicity to promote Heston's new film project on Murrow's popular *Person to Person* show. Heston (who also owned homes in Hollywood and in Wisconsin) had just returned from Egypt to star in Cecile B. DeMille's epic *The Ten Commandments*, which, even before its release, was getting a lot of attention for how much money was spent on its over-the-top production. While the movie star and his attractive wife were understandably telegenic, it was Heston's baby son, Fraser, who stole the show. In the movie, the baby played the infant Moses, reportedly signing his film contract with an imprint of his foot.[316]

BAD TO WORSE

Fortunately (for the show's sound engineer, anyway), Heston's penthouse apartment was twenty-two stories up in the air, enough distance perhaps to not hear the racket going on down below. With his loathing for automobiles and the traffic and noise they created in a congested urban environment, Fred French might have been rolling in his grave if he had been able to see and hear the vehicular conditions in and around Tudor City. As the finishing touches were being put on Tudor City Gardens, an anti-noise committee was formed to protest what it described as the "unnecessary, unlawful, disturbing, nerve-wracking and inexcusable" din being generated in the community and surrounding area. Taxis, buses, cars and the Consolidated Edison plant located at 38th Street and First Avenue were the primary culprits, according to the group, with some 1,500 residents signing a supportive petition the committee had placed in the lobbies of the twelve buildings. The petition asked Mayor Robert F. Wagner and Police Commissioner Francis W.H. Adams to "enforce existing laws prohibiting unnecessary horn-blowing" and, should that fail, that citizens be deputized to help manage the situation.[317]

While the sources of the clamor were disparate, it was the Unique Garage on 44th Street that appeared to be the biggest and loudest problem. Many a commuter arrived at the garage between 5:00 a.m. and 7:00 a.m. in the morning and honked their respective horn to gain entrance, waking many residents whose apartments were in buildings on the north side of the community. Judging by a poem one resident had written regarding the noise in the general area, the honking of horns on or near Tudor City Place was a problem at night as well. "The horn blew at midnight and all through the house, it scared all the people and even a mouse," went one verse, with seventeen additional verses leaving no doubt that the poet did not appreciate cars making themselves heard in the wee hours. Others found the roar of buses or rumbling from Con Ed's electrical plant (which predated Tudor City, having been built in 1902) as the most cacophonous, but all agreed that one of the community's biggest selling points—its quiet—had largely vanished.[318]

Of course, Tudor City was hardly the only community in Manhattan experiencing noise and environmental problems in the 1950s. It would be another decade for citizens' concerns about the quality of life in the city to gel into a legitimate movement, but signs of a growing discontent with the failure of lawmakers to take action could already be detected. A new activist group called Committee for a Quiet City was formed in 1957 to address the noise issue, with Charles Hunt of the Manor representing Tudor City's stake in the matter. A certain critical mass was also forming with regard to the soot problem, evidenced by this excerpt from a July 1957 *New York Times* editorial titled "Time for War on Grime":

> *Complaints, reports are no solution*
> *For our war on air pollution.*
> *Our smoke has gone from bad to worse.*
> *Our housewives now lament in verse....*[319]

With no action resulting from their 1955 petition protesting the noise problem in the community, Tudor City residents generated a new one that addressed the soot issue as well. A group calling itself the Committee for a Cleaner, Quieter Tudor City sent another petition to Mayor Wagner in September 1957, with 1,855 residents making known their unhappiness with the city's response (or lack thereof). The redevelopment of 42nd Street as part of the improved approach to the UN (which ended up costing about $25 million, or about $235 million today) was undoubtedly an impressive feat of engineering, this petition explained, but it had major acoustic consequences for the people who lived in the area.[320] Just as intended, significantly more traffic could now pass through the underpass of the new bridge on Tudor City Place, but these vehicles were creating a level of noise that, when amplified by the tunnel, became a full-fledged roar. If that were not enough, managers of the nearby Con Ed plant would occasionally release steam into the air when the pressure built up to a certain degree, the result being a loud blast that rattled residents' windows and made their walls shake.[321]

Three members of this latest activist group were not content to wait for Mayor Wagner to do something to make Tudor City cleaner and quieter. These residents all happened to be engineers (one chemical, one electrical and one mechanical) and thus had some expertise in the environmental effects of producing energy from coal. The trio requested a meeting with Con Ed to see for themselves what was causing both the noise and soot that were making the lives of many Tudor City residents miserable. Surprisingly, rather than get the typical corporate brushoff when making such a request, Con Ed was happy to oblige. The company had a public relations problem, after all, and viewed a meeting with the engineers as an opportunity to demonstrate the complexities of creating massive amounts of electricity. Also surprisingly, rather than bringing back a scathing attack on Con Ed's procedures, the three engineers were on the whole very impressed with the company's operations. The trio inspected the plant along with Con Ed's engineers (and PR team) and returned quite satisfied with the company's efforts to keep noise and soot to a minimum. The truth was that until a new, "cleaner" form of energy (such as natural gas) could be sourced, the burning of coal would have a negative environmental impact in a densely populated city like New York. It was also important to keep in mind that there were many other contributing factors to what would soon be called "air pollution," not the least being that 86 million exhaust-emitting vehicles crossed the city's bridges and tunnels annually.[322]

Yet one more annoyance, at least for some Tudor City residents, was the recent arrival of homeless and economically disadvantaged people asking passersby for money. Stone benches had been placed on 42nd Street behind Tudor and Prospect Towers as part of the improvements for the UN area, attracting panhandlers from the Bowery and other parts of the city. Such folks were also making their way onto Tudor City Place and tailing tenants as they walked toward the lobbies of their respective buildings, something Eberle found particularly vexing. "Are you helping to perpetuate this begging nuisance?" he asked readers in 1958, urging residents to not give them money so that they would hopefully go away.[323]

WORDS OF PRAISE

While Tudor City residents struggled with irritating intrusions from the outside world in the late '50s, they took comfort in the fact that, in some ways, the community was better than ever. A prime example was the Tudor City School, which, after its formation a half century earlier, had become nationally recognized for its innovative methods and academic excellence. Edna Travers, who had founded the school with the opening of Tudor City in 1927, had recently died, but the school was carrying on with a new director and a growing number of students. As a private institution (yet also public in that it served children in a dedicated, local community), the school was seen as offering the best of both worlds in elementary education. It is "the most enviably unique institution of its kind in this part of the country," said one child psychologist about the school, quite an accolade given its humble beginnings.[324] The city's baby boom was also leading to the opening of new schools for Tudor City's young people. The Walt Whitman School on East 43rd Street and the Baruch Junior High School on 20th Street between First and Second Avenues each opened in 1956, allowing students to receive their education closer to where they lived.[325]

Another reason to be happy about the current state of Tudor City was that its two parks had been wonderfully restored and were, arguably, more beautiful than ever. A prominent landscaper had been brought in to reimagine the parks after the twenty-two-foot strip had been snatched by the city, and everyone was delighted with the results. Ten different kinds of trees—sycamore, linden, Norway maple, flowering cherry, pin oak, flowering crabapple, ash, catalpa, magnolia and alanthus—could now be found in the parks, which remained a source of joy for the many tenants who regularly walked its paths, ate lunch on its benches or just took in some sun.[326] Herman Kessler (just "Herman" to residents) had served as the gardener of the parks since 1950, and he was given ample, deserved credit for their appearance following Robert Moses's theft a decade earlier. Herman was also well known to patrol the grounds and ask unfamiliar faces in which apartment they lived, with a wrong answer (a number and letter combination that did not match those in any of the buildings) earning trespassers a prompt removal from the still private parks.

Perhaps the greatest tribute to Tudor City these years came from resident Richard Joseph, who happened to be the travel editor of *Esquire* magazine. Joseph traveled the world for his job and, with his nice salary, could live almost wherever he wanted in or around the city, but he chose Tudor City for the same reasons many others in the community did. In the December 1958 issue of the hip men's publication, Joseph described Tudor City as a kind of village within the city, with a small-town atmosphere offering its residents a true sense of place. There was a village green (the two private parks), a post office, a collection of little shops (including a cobbler), a main street (Tudor City Place) and a modestly sized school—all things one would associate more with a rural community than midtown Manhattan. Fred French likely did not know Walt Disney, but the design of Tudor City in some respects resembled that of recently built Disneyland, which also aspired to provide the feeling that one was in a small town populated by friendly and happy people.[327]

Others had "words of praise for Tudor City," as Eberle described Joseph's article, helping to put all the recent bad news about the place in perspective. Just as French had said thirty years earlier, city folks who had left Manhattan for the suburbs might have regrets when the realities of going back and forth sunk in. The late '50s were not good ones for New York City commuter trains, as the costs to run and maintain them exceeded revenues on most suburban lines. (With fewer trains and passengers, some operators were actually on the verge of bankruptcy.) Driving to and from Manhattan was no joy either during the golden age of the automobile, with traffic jams somewhere along the route routinely ruining whatever plans had been made. As in the mid-'50s, when Tudor City Gardens opened its doors for business, suburbanites who had grown weary of the commute were choosing that particular building as their new home. In May 1959, the *New York Herald Tribune* interviewed two such couples who had recently moved to the building, which had gained no fewer than thirty-three new tenants in the previous year from the suburbs.[328]

With the help of Tudor City, Manhattan was getting back some of the 200,000 or so New Yorkers who had left for the suburbs over the last decade.

As a modern building, and the only one in Tudor City that had significant numbers of apartments to fill, it made sense that those who relocated to Westchester and Connecticut and missed Manhattan were handpicking Tudor City Gardens as the place to live. The East midtown neighborhood was also a draw, especially with the changes that it had experienced over the past fifteen years. The Second Avenue "el" was gone and the UN had been built, with a cluster of other international organizations springing up around it. 42nd Street had been redeveloped, and new buildings were going up on the corner of that street and Second Avenue. In Tudor City, the old tennis courts were now the site of the first apartment building to be put up in the community in a quarter of a century, and was the final piece in Fred French's ambitious "scientific rebuilding of Manhattan."[329]

Words of praise for Tudor City—or at least for urban life in general—also came from, of all sources, the American Medical Association. In a 1959 article in that association's journal, the authors challenged the popular postwar notion that life in suburbia was an attractive alternative to the trials and tribulations to be found in most American cities. The suburbs were hardly the Eden-like paradise they were commonly believed to be, the authors' research showed, with a host of challenges, including commuting, home maintenance and improvement (especially lawn care), high taxes and a competitive form of consumption often found there. The worse news was that the combination of these stresses was leading to more heart attacks, ulcers and hypertension among both male and female suburbanites than urbanites, a surprising finding.[330] One had to ask after reading the article: were the suburbs hazardous to one's health? Perhaps it was in the best interests of those living or considering moving there to rethink their decision. The article did not go that far, but it did reinforce Fred French's intuition that city life offered distinct advantages over the supposed utopian suburbs. Urban America, especially New York City, was on the brink of experiencing a transformation that French could never have anticipated, however, demanding that Tudor City reinvent itself yet again.

Chapter 4

FALLING APART, 1960–1975

These small parks [in Tudor City] *are an irreplaceable amenity in congested midtown.*
—October 4, 1972 editorial in the New York Times

On Wednesday, July 26, 1972, approximately five hundred residents of Tudor City gathered in the community's parks. It was Tudor City's forty-fifth "birthday," but the people were not there to celebrate the opening of the development's first two buildings in 1927. Rather, the group consisted of members of the Save Our Parks Committee, a tenant organization formed by John P. McKean whose goal was to stop the new owner of Tudor City from constructing a new luxury apartment building (or possibly two) on the site. In place of throwing a birthday party for Tudor City, the group was holding a "Farewell Party" to the parks as a way to "dramatize their fears that next year there would perhaps be no park," as a reporter for the *New York Times* expressed it. A number of elected officials, including Representative Edward Koch, whose Congressional district encompassed Tudor City, were there to show support for the organization. Also there was eighty-five-year-old Jeannette Seidman, who had been a resident of Tudor City since the ticker-tape parade was held for Charles Lindbergh's flight across the Atlantic and when *The Jazz Singer* was playing in local movie theaters. "I've lived here for 45 years and it's been a lovely time and it would kill the old people if Mr. Helmsley took away our park," Seidman said, speaking of the man who planned to cover the green space with a concrete tower.[331]

Like New York City, New York State and the country as a whole, Tudor City went through great change during the tumultuous 1960s and early 1970s, as social, political and economic forces took the community in a new direction. New York was "falling apart," one resident of the city observed in 1971, a sentiment many shared as a recession and rising crime rate turned the town into a more run-down and dangerous place. As with Gotham itself, it was clear that one chapter of Tudor City's history had ended and another had begun, this new one heavily defined by conflict and contentiousness. While Tudor City had settled into a relative comfort zone in the 1950s after the thorny arrival of its new neighbor the United Nations, the counterculture era would be ridden with clashes with the city and with real estate developers who had other ideas for the community.

Inspired perhaps by a very active protest scene in New York City and on college campuses across the country in the late 1960s and early 1970s—much of it centered on the Vietnam War and discrimination against women, gays and African Americans—residents of Tudor City rose up in considerable numbers to fight for their own causes. The UN remained a perceived threat, with fears that the world organization would encroach on its neighboring village. The environmental movement was also heating up in the late '60s, motivation for tenants to do whatever they could to protect and preserve their small but beloved green space that was in particular jeopardy. The city within a city would come under major attack during these years, but those calling Tudor City home were prepared to do battle.

A SIZABLE DELEGATION

It was undeniably an exciting time for the city and the nation as the 1960s began, with much hope that the Cold War tensions of the last decade would ease. Much of the efforts of Tudor City's next-door neighbor were being directed toward that very pursuit, with east midtown Manhattan as a whole developing into a district dedicated to making the world a better and safer place. The UN had altered the fabric of the neighborhood beyond its physical infrastructure in a way that Fred French could not anticipated but likely would have appreciated. "With the United Nations Organization as a magnet," Warren Eberle observed in his *Tudor City View* in March 1960, "this neighborhood is rapidly becoming a center for agencies and organizations that are seeking to promote better human understanding as a means of achieving a more friendly and peaceful world." Indeed, a number of such institutions—including the American Field Service, the Foundation for Continuing Education (part of the Ford Foundation), the Boys Clubs of America, the U.S. Missions to the UN, the Foreign Policy Association and World Brotherhood Inc. (located on the second floor of Tudor Hotel)—had arrived in the area over the last few years, with more likely on the way.[332]

While it was certainly nice that Tudor City had, through no effort of its own, found itself part of a whole neighborhood geared toward international goodwill, there were definite downsides to being so close to the literal action. Every year, from late September to mid-October, the area was invaded by hordes of New York City's finest as heads of state made appearances at the UN. Many police officers and other law enforcement officials—too many, Tudor City residents felt—were assigned to the broader area, primarily to protect communist leaders from crowds.[333] Beyond the problem of getting in and out of the community by foot or car, the autumnal meetings of the General Assembly created additional havoc for residents (and still do). Parking had been limited to one side of Tudor City Place since its widening a decade or so earlier, but beginning in 1960, the police started to use the west side of the street to park their squad cars when guarding UN VIPs. It was that year that Cuban prime minister Fidel Castro and Soviet premier Nikita Khrushchev came to town, with law enforcement believing that additional security was required to guard the two most important representatives of the Communist Party.[334] "Looking back over the UN's special sessions and anniversary celebrations, an early one—the fifteenth, in 1960—provided a month of drama and chaos that New Yorkers would talk about for years," Pamela Hanlon wrote in her *A Worldly Affair*, with Khrushchev and Castro two of the thirty world leaders who turned the city upside down at the height of the Cold War.[335]

It was understandable how, with extra police needed for such special occasions, Tudor City residents would have to put up with some inconveniences for a few weeks given the proximity of the community to the UN. After that year's General Assembly meeting, however, the city's Traffic Department posted signs allowing two-side (west and east) parking on Tudor City Place, something that most residents did not like at all. Commuters to the nearby midtown business district were grabbing the parking spaces and leaving their cars there all day, for one thing, and with more traffic, crossing the street had become more dangerous for pedestrians. Also, one of the reasons given for the narrowing of the parks alongside Tudor City Place was that fire trucks couldn't turn around on the street, but now, with two-side parking, the same problem was back. One could now reasonably conclude that the parkland had been taken for, well, parking, completely consistent with Robert Moses's reputation for prioritizing automobiles over people.[336]

The presence of the UN brought other annoyances to residents of Tudor City. Protests in the area could get loud enough for tenants to easily hear, especially when a big crowd gathered or when megaphones were involved. Demonstrations also occasionally spilled over into the community itself, turning Tudor City Place into something much different than the "quiet enclave" it was typically described as. Shortly after the botched Bay of Pigs invasion of Cuba in April 1961, for example, a pro-Castro demonstration was held right behind Tudor and Prospect Towers, with Tudor City residents more likely to hear the group's chanting than the UN delegates working a few blocks north on First Avenue. (Eberle, whose politics clearly leaned right, believed that most of the demonstrators—local college students, he reckoned, judging by their logoed T-shirts—were being paid to be there.) 46th or 47th Street would have been a much better choice of location, he felt, not just because he and other tenants would then not have heard the pseudo-Commies, but because the people who actually mattered would have.[337]

A new president was in the White House, but the Cold War was as chilly as ever, sustaining New Yorkers' fears that they might be attacked by Russia. It was not reassuring to learn that the superpower was testing atomic bombs in 1961 and, perhaps worse, that the city's temperate zone was in the direct line of fallout from such bombs. In other words, even if the Soviet Union chose another part of the world to attack, say Europe, the residue from a mushroom cloud was likely to eventually drift over Manhattan Island. Homeowners in the suburbs were able to build bomb shelters should such a thing happen, but that offered little comfort to more anxious apartment dwellers. "Certain nervous residents of Tudor City have appealed to the Management to provide shelters for relief from strontium-90," Eberle reported in October of that year, with these folks thinking that having a fallout-proof room in each of the building's basements would be a valuable addition to the community given the uncertain times.[338]

While Tudor City residents worried that World War III might be arriving on their doorsteps at any moment, there were the mundane problems of urban life to deal with. Some television watchers in the community were seeing snow rather than their favorite shows on a few of their channels, the cause being the steel framework going up in the thirty-three-story Pfizer Building on Second Avenue and 42nd Street, as well as the forty-one-story Continental Can Building at Third Avenue and 41st Street. Those buildings were located in between Tudor City and the Empire State Building's tower, on which television antennae were placed.[339] Another minor irritation was the recent arrival of a flock of unwelcome guests to the two parks. "A sizable delegation of Bryant Park pigeons has moved in on our Tudor City Parks," Eberle noted in the summer of 1961, the birds wisely choosing the fecund lawns on which to feed.[340]

As park lovers watched where they walked and sat, French Company executives pondered the future of the three-decade-old development. Reconfiguring the makeup of Tudor City was the company's first order of business in the early 1960s. About 7,500 people now lived in the immediate community, and with no more land there on which to build, the company had to look in the surrounding area if it was to continue to grow. While it would not be located in Tudor City proper, a new, eighteen-story office building was springing up along Second Avenue between 41st and 42nd Streets (abutting the Tudor City Hotel) in 1962 and 1963; this would be the company's first office building in the broader area.[341]

Finding anywhere to build in east midtown was getting increasingly difficult for the French Company and other private developers as the presence of the United Nations attracted other globally oriented organizations to the area. First Avenue in particular had been transformed over the past decade, as a bevy of modern office buildings sprang up along what was called United Nations Plaza, the six-block portion of that avenue running from East 42nd to East 48th Streets.[342] Top executives of many corporations were also deciding that locating their headquarters within walking distance of the UN (and perhaps Tudor City) lent a certain status. Between 1951 (when the UN's Secretariat Building was completed) and 1963, eight skyscrapers had risen on East 42nd Street, adding about 4 million square feet of office space to that part of Manhattan.[343]

The UN campus had raised the bar in modern architecture and was obviously serving as inspiration for the design of all new buildings in the area. The French Company's new metal (bronze-toned aluminum) and glass (and air-conditioned) tower was far more modern than Tudor City Gardens, which had been added to Tudor City in the mid-1950s and had nothing at all to do with the sixteenth-century style of architecture that Fred French had borrowed in creating the other ten apartment buildings and hotel in the late '20s. The French Company had not put up a commercial structure since erecting the Fred F. French Building on Fifth Avenue in 1927, quite a lapse of time, but taking that corner made a lot of sense. The Pfizer Building, the Daily News Annex and 800 Second Avenue took up the three other corners, each one an office building that had risen in the past few years.

Rentals would be handled not by the French Company but by Helmsley Spear, which had expertise in the commercial side of the business.[344]

Management changes at the company likely had something to do with the new direction it was going. Ferdinand Roth was now acting as president of the French Company's investing group, and William H. Robb was appointed as the new executive manager of Tudor City in 1963.[345] That same year, the Tudor City Hotel (which actually consisted of two buildings with a common lobby and basement) was sold, as management decided to focus on its primary business of real estate. Modernizing and redecorating the hotel would be the new investor group's priority, as the 575 rooms, restaurant and banquet and meeting facilities looked every bit their thirty-plus years of age.[346] The French Company was hardly the only real estate developer in the city going out with the old and in with the new in the early '60s. Real estate values were rising dramatically due to a new wave of construction (and inflation), encouraging all developers to manage their portfolio of holdings closely. Not unrelatedly, Manhattan had become the international capital of the world in finance, art and other arenas after the war, bringing more attention to the fact that land was a finite (and thus increasingly valuable) resource on the island.

A FILE OF BLUE

A less glamorous side of the real estate business was the day-to-day management of operating a giant apartment complex. Residents were told to keep the volume down on their televisions, radios and hi-fis, especially in the warmer months when windows were open, so as not to disturb their neighbors.[347] "Don't allow strangers into your apartment" went another piece of advice, this following an incident when a woman was robbed after letting in someone she didn't know.[348] After a number of fires in trash rooms, tenants were warned to close the doors of incinerators, lest more blazes occur. Last, residents were asked to turn off their air conditioners when going out, as these electricity-gobbling machines cost the French Company a good deal of money now that many residents owned them.[349]

All this routine housekeeping represented the proverbial calm before the storm, however, as a more chaotic cultural climate began to envelop Tudor City. In September 1964, residents learned that they would have another prominent neighbor, this one the Ford Foundation (the largest foundation in the country). Over the next three years, a twelve-story structure would be going up on 42nd and 43rd Streets between First and Second Avenues, just west of Tudor City. The building, designed by Eero Saarinen Associates (the eponymous architect himself had recently died), would "depart radically from routine New York office construction and promises to add a distinguished landmark to the United Nations neighborhood," Ada Louise Huxtable wrote in the *New York Times*, clearly delighted by the unveiled plans.[350] Architectural critics would rave about the stone and glass building when it opened in 1967, especially its indoor garden that contained thousands of permanent trees, shrubs, vines and other greenery. "The warm granite facing blends with the colors of the Tudor City development nearby," wrote Steven V. Roberts of the *New York Times*, thinking that the architects did indeed take into account the character of the neighborhood as they had promised.[351]

While the disturbance stemming from the construction of the new Ford Foundation building to the west was no cause for joy, the one originating from the east was considerably worse. Sewer work on First Avenue that had begun in 1965 and continued well into the following year was causing residents major grief, with the noise and dust emanating from the project the basis for many letters of complaints to Mayor Wagner and other city officials. Over that same period, a heliport was allowed to operate on the roof of the nearby Pan Am Building, with dozens of choppers arriving from and departing to Idlewild Airport every day. (Trips to and from Teterboro Airport in New Jersey would start soon as well, but unlike Idlewild, that airport was west of Tudor City, so helicopters would not go over the community.) If those two annoyances were not enough, the parking problem on Tudor City Place had gotten worse, with residents waiting for hours to get a spot and taxis unable to get close to the curb to pick up or drop off passengers.[352]

Such inconveniences, however, paled in comparison to situations in which Tudor City residents found themselves in the eye of the storm. Longtime tenants had observed many protests, as well as the sometimes frenetic comings and goings of UN people, since the organization's arrival in Turtle Bay in 1951, but the pandemonium that took place on April 15, 1967, surpassed even the time in 1960 when Khrushchev and Castro showed up. A crowd of at least 100,000 people (some estimated several hundred thousand) gathered in the Sheep Meadow of Central Park to protest the country's involvement in the Vietnam War, with many of them (including Dr. Martin Luther King, Stokely Carmichael, Harry Belafonte and Dr. Benjamin Spock) then making their way southeast to the UN's Dag Hammarskjold Plaza. (A few hundred protesters had burned their draft cards.) The demonstration was organized by the Spring Mobilization to End the War in Vietnam, a group described

Section of the massive Ford Foundation building, a close neighbor to Tudor City. *Photo by Piero Ribelli.*

by Maurice Isserman, a history professor and coauthor of *America Divided: The Civil War of the 1960s*, as "a recently assembled coalition of radical, pacifist and student groups." (This was the then sixteen-year-old Isserman's first antiwar protest.)[353]

Thousands of law enforcement officials who were instructed to report for "parade duty" that day added to the general mayhem in the area. "More than 3,000 men were assigned to maintain a file of blue between marchers and spectators," Maurice Carroll of the *Times* reported the following day, with leaders of the force asking even those who had desk jobs to put on uniforms to make their presence felt. Representatives of the FBI, UN security force and the city's Housing Authority and Transit Authority were also on site wearing civilian clothes and small lapels indicating for whom they worked.[354] Such a large group of law enforcement people was needed given that a counterdemonstration was taking place at the same time a few blocks south. About one thousand supporters of the war (some of them the Young Americans for Freedom) converged on First Avenue directly across the UN to push for the United States to escalate its involvement in the conflict, briefly interrupting their patriotic chanting to jeer Martin Luther King Jr. as he entered the main building after speaking at the protestors' rally.[355]

With Tudor City so close to this bedlam, it is not surprising that a portion of it spilled over into the community. Tenants whose apartments overlooked Tudor City Place could see hundreds of marchers on their main street carrying signs, a source of joy for those who supported the antiwar movement and something completely different among those (including the conservative Eberle) who believed that such demonstrations were simply giving comfort to the enemy (i.e., Communists).[356] A good number of the police remained in the general area until late in the evening in case trouble broke out after the demonstration, further making the experience an unforgettable one for those who lived in the neighborhood.[357] The day must have been a particularly trying one for New Yorkers whose sons or daughters were currently serving in the military in Southeast Asia. There were, in fact, a number of residents of Tudor City who were presently in Vietnam, and a few French Company employees were there as well. Some of these soldiers, sailors and pilots had grown up in Tudor City, a place they undoubtedly wished they would one day see again.

Like a Village

The UN would continue to directly affect the lives of Tudor City residents. One year after the massive protest, residents of Tudor City learned that there were plans to expand the UN into a "campus," complete with tall towers, parks and walkways. Governor Rockefeller and Mayor Lindsay had recently shown support for adding the two-block area west of First Avenue between 43rd and 45th Streets to the organization's site, extending the redevelopment of the midtown east neighborhood that had begun forty years earlier with the creation of Tudor City. A complex of offices, luxury apartments, a hotel and a restaurant would replace the current warehouses, garages and loft buildings—an urban renewal plan that appeared to be inspired by the one that had led to the development of Lincoln Center on the Upper West Side.[358]

Although the possible creation of a larger United Nations campus made no mention of annexing Tudor City, some tenants again believed that the powers that be were thinking of grabbing additional land from its residential neighbor. (This despite the fact that the UN was having financial problems, and if there was any kind of transaction, some quipped, it would be the French Company buying the world organization's campus.)[359] Still, fearing that they might soon be evicted, about 150 residents of Tudor City and some others who lived nearby picketed in front of the recently completed Ford Foundation building in December 1968. The Ford Foundation had contributed $100,000 to the Fund for Area Planning and Development (as had the Rockefeller Brothers Fund), making its building a good place for the protesters—most of them older women—to gather. Some of the picket signs read, "Let us have our homes in peace and not in pieces," reflecting the concern that Tudor City's now forty-year-old buildings would be knocked down and replaced by a set of modern structures much like the glass-and-granite Ford Foundation building.[360]

Leading the protest was John F. McKean, a real estate executive and resident of Tudor City with plenty of experience in property law that would come in very handy. For the next two and a half decades, McKean would play a heroic role in preserving the community as "a refuge from the clamor of modern life," as a 1929 advertisement had referred to Tudor City. When McKean retired in 1973, he formed the Tudor City Tenants Association, a group that was a thorn in the side of anyone who in some way threatened to reduce the quality of life in the community. (A plaque was put up in McKean's honor in the North Park a year following his death in 1993.) "We're not against the U.N. development," McKean told a reporter while on the picket line at the Ford

Foundation in 1968, "but pushing people out of their homes and places of business is no good." Some of the picketers believed that the Ford Foundation planned to buy Tudor City lock, stock and barrel and perhaps donate it to the UN, much like the Rockefellers had done with the slaughterhouse district back in 1946. There was speculation that the ultimate aim for the Fund for Area Planning and Development was to turn the entire neighborhood into a "UN dormitory" that would perhaps encompass as much as ten blocks. The Foundation denied it had such plans, but Tudor City residents remained wary, knowing that their proximity to "the center of the world" made them vulnerable to the whims of the rich and powerful.[361]

City officials were by the late 1960s directing more energy to zoning in the five boroughs as real estate became more valuable and as more players entered the scene. At the same time, preservations were attempting to save what was remaining of older New York, leading to an escalating battle with developers. It was not surprising that given the size, location and history of Tudor City, city planners took a close look at its zoning status. In 1969, the City Planning Commission made a zoning change to preserve Tudor City as a residential community and protect a few of the buildings from possible demolition for new office space. Residents of Tudor City (and members of the Turtle Bay Association) had vigorously appealed to the commission for the protective status, quite understandably so given Robert Moses's snatching of twenty-two feet from its two parks two decades earlier. (A "superbuilding" was now being proposed to expand the UN's campus; this "slab city" would tower over Tudor City if constructed, with yet another plan to put a three-acre park and eight-story office building in that space along the East River.)[362] The commission's decision was subject to approval by the Board of Estimate, making residents keep their fingers crossed that this governmental body made of the city's top elected officials would agree.[363]

While the UN would indeed expand, no Tudor City residents would be forced out, the Board of Estimate decided in June 1970, giving the community a victory in its escalating battle for preservation. However, a new and even larger threat appeared with the purchase of the complete Tudor City development (except the Tudor City Gardens building, the Tudor Hotel and the new office building on Second Avenue) that same month by a group of investors (the Ramsgate Company) led by Harry B. Helmsley of Helmsley-Spear Inc. The sale price was $36 million, just what it had cost Fred French to build it in the late 1920s, although another $28 million in mortgage debt came with the deal. Helmsley assured nervous tenants that things would remain the same, but it was not entirely clear what he and his syndicate had in mind for the future of Tudor City. The French Company had consistently maintained that there was no more vacant land on which to construct additional buildings, but Helmsley believed there was. In the 1960s, Helmsley had purchased the Empire State, Graybar, Fisk and Flatiron Buildings, earning him a reputation as an aggressive developer not afraid to take chances. (More recently, Helmsley had bought the Parkchester development in the Bronx that, with twelve thousand apartments, was about four times bigger than Tudor City.) Many residents reasonably wondered what would happen to Tudor City under the ownership of real estate magnate Harry Helmsley; its purchase had triggered the most apprehension since the midcentury appearance of the United Nations.[364]

The transfer of ownership of Tudor City to a group of savvy investors from the people who had built the place four decades earlier was indeed cause for considerable unease, particularly for those who had called it home for many years. More than a quarter of residents had lived in their apartments for fifteen years or longer, with a good number of them there since the Great Depression. A fair share of tenants were paying less than $80 per month for their rent-controlled, one-room studio, seemingly too good of a deal for Helmsley, who was at least part owner of hundreds of properties in the city, to continue offering. (One-and-a-half-room apartments had been rent-controlled at $130 per month, but the recently passed New York Rent Stabilization Law of 1969 had allowed Helmsley-Spear to raise that number to as much as $300.)[365] While Tudor City was now protected from any kind of major redevelopment in the area—including the rumored construction of a giant complex between 43rd and 45th Streets along First Avenue to be orchestrated by the city, the state and the UN—residents worried that their enclave might soon be surrounded by a set of much taller buildings. The fresh breezes coming from the East River, the sunshine to be had from the open space and the largely unobstructed view had always been nice perks of Tudor City that differentiated it from other parts of the city, making the thought of a wall of forty-story office towers across the street a rather unpleasant one.[366]

A quick tour of the Tudor City neighborhood could have very well suggested that the "vacant property" Helmsley had in mind for possible development was the two still private parks. The parks, each now about 100 feet by 230 feet, remained the community's crown jewels, one might say, and a key reason why residents loved the place. "It's just minutes away from the rat race," a woman sitting in one of the parks told a reporter for the *New York Times* in October 1971, thinking that the green space was essential to making Tudor City seem "like a village." This time it was the Ford Foundation that might buy the parkland in order to relocate from its current location just west of Tudor City, residents feared, this despite the fact that top executives of the foundation denied such claims. Not helping matters were comments made to the media by Harry Helmsley, who was perhaps sending a message to potential buyers that the park property was for sale. "We are certainly exploring all possibilities," Helmsley said, adding, "I can't afford to buy a park and pay taxes on it." These were hardly reassuring words to the many residents who sat in the parks every day, weather permitting.[367]

Fortunately, residents hoping that Tudor City would stay just as it was had an ally on their side: Representative Edward L. Koch, whose district included the community. Koch had ambitious political plans and was siding with his local constituency, knowing that it represented an important voter base. Many of the residents of the community were now older people, who tended to vote in high numbers. (Assemblyman Andrew Stein, State Senator Roy M. Goodman and Manhattan Borough president Percy E. Sutton also opposed Helmsley's building plans in Tudor City.) Tudor City residents had historically leaned decidedly Republican, but the community's political slant was in the early 1970s shifting left. As evidence, the neighborhood voted in considerable numbers for the conservative Republican James Buckley (brother of William F.) in the 1970 election for United States senator, but it also sided heavily with the liberal Democrat Andrew Stein in the race for State Assembly. Tudor City constituents "tend to be intelligent and conservative, but they're not really mobilized unless there is a specific problem," Stein noted, summarizing their political philosophy as "live and live."[368]

With a greater percentage of older people in Tudor City than in previous eras, it was perhaps understandable how many residents seemed resistant to any major changes that Harry Helmsley might bring about. ("Their life-style involves a strong feeling for the way New York was," Stein also had observed of Tudor City dwellers.) The single professional class of the 1930s, military personnel of the 1940s and young families of the 1950s were now long gone, and with the baby boom over, very few children now lived in Tudor City. (Rather incredibly, just one child reportedly lived in Tudor Tower, a five-year-old girl named Debbie.) However, the new stabilization law was serving as the impetus for some older residents to leave and for new tenants, mostly upper-middle-class young couples, to take their place. While La Bibliotheque, the current restaurant in Tudor City (whose menus were printed on reproductions of *Le Monde*, the French newspaper), catered to that demographic (who would soon be labeled "yuppies"), UN officials and businesspeople from the midtown area were most likely to frequent the eatery in the Tudor Hotel. The latter restaurant had retained the Tudor theme in décor and by employing pseudo–Olde English on its menu. Managers of the place were clearly going against the grain of early '70s hipness, offering diners such items as "stake slices," "taters," "sallett," "chyken" and "juice of the tamata."[369]

Bad Policy

While Helmsley had initially said that little would change at Tudor City under his leadership, a different tone from that set by the French Company could now be easily detected. Besides being amenable to selling off pieces of property if the price were high enough, the new landlord did not hesitate evicting tenants who were behind in rent. Irene Phillips was an eighty-two-year-old woman with a serious heart condition who had lived in the Essex House since 1940, but that did not stop Helmsley-Spear from filing an eviction order in November 1971 after she forgot to pay rent for two consecutive months. With the changes made to rent control, Helmsley could now rent out her six-room apartment for twice the $169 per month she had been paying. (With such heartless maneuvers, Helmsley was well on the way to resembling Henry F. Potter from the 1946 film *It's a Wonderful Life*, but the man, who had just divorced his first wife and would soon marry Leona "Queen of Mean" Roberts, obviously did not care much about his public image.) "It's all falling apart, isn't it?" a passerby said as she saw the woman's furniture being put on the street, speaking in general of the changes taking place in New York City, and not for the better.[370]

Helmsley had yet to show his cards as the Department of Sanitation put Phillips's furniture on the sidewalk, but that did not stop two hundred residents of Tudor City from gathering in one of the two parks they feared would not exist much longer. Huddling together in the cold, the group discussed what steps they could possibly take should the new owner of the development decide to put up one or two buildings on the site. Happily, local politicians were coming forward to lend support to the tenants. Councilwoman Carol Greitzer stopped by to say, "I'll do all I can to help you," and Stanley Richman, council to State Senator Roy Goodman, also made a brief appearance to let the group know that the Republican representing the borough of Manhattan was on their side.[371]

The disappointing news that Helmsley did indeed intend to construct high-rise buildings on the site of the two parks was more proof that New York was not the city it used to be. New York had always been a city that looked more to the future than the past, but the 1970s were setting a new bar in terms of discarding the old for the new. The decade was also turning out to be a prime time for social activism, however, and Tudor City residents had every intention of fighting back. Led by John McKean, chair of the five-hundred-member Save Our Parks Committee, Tudor City began a campaign in late 1971 to save its parks from being destroyed and the space used for new apartment houses. (A sidebar to Helmsley's plan was that forty thousand square feet would be set aside for a "park-like" open space that would be made public, a means perhaps of appeasing angry tenants and, more importantly, lowering or eliminating taxes on that piece of property.)[372] Rezoning the park areas (from R-10 to R-3) by the City Planning Commission would make it much more costly to build new buildings on the site, however, making this the strategy the committee chose to try to stop the development. Five local lawmakers—Koch, Stein and Goodman along with City Council members Carter Burden and Carol Greitzer—backed McKean's plan, issuing a statement saying as much. "The conversion of park land into concrete edifices in mid-Manhattan is bad policy," the statement read, with "the traffic congestion which would inevitably follow…[likely to] destroy the sense of tranquility which has historically existed within Tudor City."[373]

Helmsley, meanwhile, was not backing down as the City Planning Commission decided what, if anything, it should do. "I have a perfect right to build on the park," he said in July 1972, "and I will do so." Development offered the possibility of getting rid of a liability on his balance sheet—the mortgage interest and taxes he had to pay on the parkland—and, at the same time, creating a revenue-generating asset. Tudor City now consisted of a dozen buildings with 3,300 apartments occupied by nearly ten thousand people, but Helmsley saw big money to be made from one new fifty-story or two twenty-eight-story luxury apartment buildings that would take up some or all of the park space. The decision by the City Planning Commission to get involved in the kerfuffle was unusual; the city had always allowed the market and, if necessary, the courts to settle such matters. Changing zoning regulations specifically to take away an owner's developmental rights was something the commission wanted to avoid doing, if only because it would almost certainly lead to legal action by Helmsley.[374]

In the spirit of the activist times (the Black Panthers had recently held a protest in New York City and Jane Fonda had just visited North Vietnam), McKean's five-hundred-member band literally made their voices heard by holding their "Farewell Party" to their parks. In addition to Koch and Sutton, Fred C. Hart, commissioner of the Department of Air Resources, and Robert N. Rickles, his predecessor and now executive director of the Institute for Public Transportation, were present and backing the Save Our Parks Committee. "Parks are absolutely essential if we are to save New York," Rickles stated, with Sutton going on the record to say that "the City Council should take prompt legislative action on the matter." It was feisty Ed Koch, however, who understood that this battle was part of a much bigger war that was taking place in the city. "It'll be an outrage if the park is demolished to make way for a high rise," the future mayor barked, seeing the situation as "really a fight for the whole city."[375]

In September 1972, the City Planning Commission made a decision regarding the clash between arguably the most powerful developer in New York City and a group of vociferous New Yorkers supported by a handful of local politicians. In yet another unusual move, the commission came up with a number of different options that would be presented in a public hearing the following month. One was to allow Helmsley to erect a forty-six-story apartment building on East 42nd Street, another being the right to put up a two-building structure over that street with traffic to run underneath (much like the Pan Am Building on Park Avenue). There were other, more complicated options as well in the proposal, at least one of which would affect one or both of Tudor City's parks. Opening up the parks to the public was now a very likely scenario, leaving Gramercy Park as the final remaining private park of note in the city.[376]

The most controversial idea would be for Helmsley to swap the parkland (valued at the time for $10 million) for a "building-density bonus," real estate lingo meaning that a financial incentive would be offered to the developer to put up a bigger and/or higher-than-currently-zoned building elsewhere. Granting Helmsley "air rights" in another part of town could entice him to give up his plan to build on the parkland, the commission believed. Never before had the commission decided to hold a public hearing to discuss options in a dispute such as this, adding another unique dimension to the history of Tudor City. After the hearing, the commission would make its recommendation, which would be subject to approval by the Board of Estimate.[377]

On the day of the public hearing, a *New York Times* editor noted the unparalleled course the Tudor City parks controversy was taking. "This is an out-of-the-ordinary hearing," the editor wrote on October 4, seeing the meeting as "an almost unprecedented municipal response to a community cry for help." While extraordinary in some sense, the situation at the same time revealed what the newspaper called "recurrent questions in the urban dilemma." How should the city—or, really, any community—

best manage private versus public interests? Should developing something new be considered a greater priority than preserving what already existed? Lawmakers in cities and towns across the country were facing such tough questions as real estate, specifically its rising value, collided with the growing preservation/conservation/environmentalism movement of the 1970s. Whatever the outcome, it was clear that a good many New Yorkers, seeing the city they knew and loved disappear bit by bit to developers like Helmsley, were drawing a line in the sand. Local activism would play a greater role in shaping the contours of the city, it was safe to say, with the fate of Tudor City's little parks to have a significant impact on future urban development.[378]

A MIGHTY STRUGGLE

For some residents of Tudor City, it was that the community's private parks would almost certainly be made public that represented the worst part of any deal made between the city and Helmsley. "The preservation of these parks should be considered as much the tenants' right as elevator service or other maintenance rights which induced us, explicitly or implicitly to rent our apartments in Tudor City in the first place," wrote George Cohen in a letter to the editor of the *Times*, clearly not happy that the city was planning to convert the green spaces from private to public. Many of the older residents of the community were frequent habitués of the parks, one reason being that, because only tenants could enter, they were essentially crime-free. The crime rate in New York City was high and still rising in the early '70s, making the parks a safe haven for those residents nervous that they might get mugged or worse once they left the neighborhood. "Derelicts and winos who are frequently to be seen in areas in or near Tudor City would find these parks, if made public, attractive places to sleep or prey upon these tenants," Cohen continued; he certainly was not the only resident who had been long dreading the day that was probably coming.[379]

While the prospect of derelicts and winos moving into Tudor City's parks was not an attractive one for residents like Cohen, the much worse possibility was that there would be no parks at all should Helmsley be allowed to turn them into a construction zone. Fortunately, in November 1972, the City Planning Commission voted to block construction of the new buildings, just one step but a very big one in the layers of government that had to be taken if residents were to keep their parks. By a 5–1 vote, the planners agreed to a zoning modification that would create a special parks district to put the brakes on Helmsley's plan, with the developer to receive in return a 20 percent bonus in building space on other properties he owned in Manhattan. The proposal still required approval by the Board of Estimate, however, reason enough for Tudor City residents to hold off on any celebration.[380]

One month later, on December 8, the Board of Estimate announced its decision: Tudor City would keep its parks, although, as it was predicted, they would be made public (between 6:00 a.m. and 10:00 p.m., presumably to deter less desirables from making them their bedrooms). As the city planners had recommended, a special park district would be created that covered the two parks, the zoning modification that McKean's committee and political allies had pushed for. "This is one of those rare situations in which members of a community have gotten together, not to exclude someone else but to save something," declared Deputy Mayor Edward Morrison following the vote. In return, Helmsley-Spear would receive comparable air rights (the ability to put up a high-rise building or buildings) in a different part of the city, something usually only awarded to preserve historical landmarks. The dozens of Tudor City residents who were in attendance while the board announced its decision (by a 20–2 vote) burst into applause and cheers. Helmsley's lawyers immediately appealed the decision, however, meaning the victory could be just a temporary one. The ruling was "impractical, unfeasible, inadvisable and unconstitutional," one attorney argued, thinking that the courts would agree that his client's property had been illegally seized.[381]

Editors for the *New York Times* believed the board's decision was "eminently fair," however, and that the swapping of the parkland for comparable air rights in another part of the city was as good a compromise that could be made. Such parks were "an endangered species," the newspaper felt, with those trying to protect them usually no match against rich and powerful developers like Helmsley and city officials who knew that higher taxes would be reaped from tall buildings on the site. The transfer of air rights would probably become more common after the Tudor City decision, editors believed, with an unlikely force—McKean's Save Our Parks Committee—doing much to push that option into municipal law. The group "waged a mighty struggle in behalf of the Tudor City sanctuaries of green, beautifully landscaped in the English manner with pebbled walks, shrubs and trees," editors wrote, clearly delighted that "these delightful parks will remain as refuges from the hurly-burly and congestion of East 42nd Street."[382]

While his lawyers continued to challenge the Board of Estimate's decision, Harry Helmsley sought other ways to parlay his purchase of Tudor City into a much bigger payday. In December 1973, the man announced that he and his syndicate would offer condominium ownership at Tudor City, with his initial proposal to the State Attorney General's Office requesting the right to put up ninety-five apartments in the Essex House for sale. Helmsley had gone a similar route at another large apartment building complex he managed, the twelve-thousand-unit Parkchester in the Bronx, where he was attempting to convert the entire development to condominiums after his initial offering of just a portion (the north quadrangle).[383] The fact that Helmsley had taken a phased approach with Parkchester was a disturbing sign that he would ultimately convert all of Tudor City from rentals to condominiums. New York City real estate history appeared to be in the making, with Tudor City again in the mix. "Mr. Helmsley's conversion plans are being widely watched both by real estate people and urban affairs experts who believe that their success could influence ownership patterns in large middle-income apartment developments generally," Joseph P. Fried wrote in the *New York Times*, recognizing that this could be the beginning of a redefinition of what constituted "home" in the city and across the nation.[384]

Right on cue, McKean and the rest of the tenant association opposed Helmsley's latest move, believing that such a move would radically change the character of Tudor City. Most of the ninety-five apartments that would be offered for sale were rent-controlled or rent-stabilized, making condominiums a means for Helmsley to make much more money much faster. (Present tenants would allegedly not be evicted if they decided not to buy their units.) There had been tenant opposition to Helmsley's plan at Parkchester as well, with the state's attorney general putting a hold on any conversion until lawsuits related to the matter were settled. (The Attorney General's Office had to approve any condominium and cooperative apartment sales.) Attorney General Louis Lefkowitz had given Helmsley the okay for his initial offering at Parkchester, after which tenants promptly filed the suit. Helmsley was doubling down there now, going to court to win approval for all apartments at Parkchester to be converted to condominiums. The case would obviously set a precedent for what would likely take place at Tudor City, with residents there (especially those in the Essex House) keeping a keen eye on what the court decided.[385]

With the Fresh Meadows development in Queens, yet another large apartment complex that Helmsley was trying to convert to condominiums, Attorney General Lefkowitz certainly had his hands full with just that one man's case file. Tenant association leaders there were also fighting the attempted conversion and called for all such efforts by landlords to be postponed until Lefkowitz came back with an overall plan. The laws relating to such matters were currently heavily stacked in landlords' favor, making McKean and other leaders of tenant groups in opposition to their development "going condo" urge the attorney general to recommend that the state legislature revisit and hopefully revise what was on the books. Approval from residents of a development was not currently needed to convert from apartment rentals to ownership, something that opposing tenants believed was unfair to the people who actually lived in the buildings.[386]

While Lefkowitz weighed his options, the Tudor City parks issue, which had seemingly been settled, got a lot more complicated. Following the Board of Estimate's decision in December 1972, Helmsley and his partners from Ramsgate decided to default on the mortgage they had acquired from the French Company when the syndicate purchased Tudor City. Left hanging with the $28 million of debt, the French Company then sued the city for its rezoning of the parks as a means to save it from Helmsley's bulldozers. (It also appeared that after Helmsley's defeat, he had stopped maintaining the parks. Even if the parks became open to the public, the deal made at the time stipulated that the owner of the property would still keep them up.) In January 1974, the New York Supreme Court declared the rezoning as unconstitutional, specifically that the Board of Estimate's decision reduced the value of the property (which was used to secure the mortgages) and that Ramsgate had been inadequately compensated.[387]

With the parks in danger once again now that the deal between the city and Helmsley appeared to be off, McKean gathered his troops for another rally. State Senator Roy Goodman had long showed support for the tenants' opposition to development, and he was there again at Tudor City in February 1974 to join this latest protest. Goodman implored the city to "vigorously appeal" the recent Supreme Court decision that declared the rezoning of the parks unconstitutional, reprising his view that two additional towers on the site would take much away from the quality of life in the community.[388] While that battle was fought, those opposed to the conversion of the ninety-five apartments in the Essex House to condominiums declared their own victory. In June 1974, Governor Malcolm Wilson signed a bill requiring that 35 percent of current tenants (including those in rent-controlled or rent-stabilized apartments) approve a proposal to convert their building into condos or co-ops, impetus for Helmsley to decide to, at least temporarily, "defer" his plan. The new law made Helmsley's proposed conversion "impractical," but the man (who was out of the country when he received the bad news) said that he would wait to see how the bill was implemented before he decided what to do next.[389]

It was fitting that, given the activism that many Tudor City residents had displayed since 1968, the community was chosen for a citywide tenant rally in December 1975. Leaders and representatives of ten tenant associations got together there to join forces by agreeing to urge residents of their respective buildings to support rent control, which appeared to be in danger because of the city's fiscal crisis.[390] New York City was, in short, broke, and the federal government had made it clear that it would not provide a bailout. In her 2017 *Fear City*, Kim Phillips-Fein documented how New York's fiscal crisis of the 1970s led to a politics of austerity, in which the so-called profligate ways of urban liberalism were blamed for the city's looming bankruptcy. The slower economic growth of the early '70s made the kind of social services that had been provided for lower-income Americans impossible, the Ford administration maintained, an idea that budget-conscious city officials were effectively forced to embrace.[391]

In great need of an influx of revenue in order for the city to stay solvent, Mayor Beame looked to the property taxes paid by landlords as a possible source of additional income. Higher rents promised the possibility of higher property taxes, and recent changes in rent control laws opened a window for Beame. Raising rents would also be consistent with the Ford administration's laissez-faire view (i.e., that the market should regulate itself rather than be controlled by the government) and with the conclusion being made by conservatives that subsidizing the lifestyles of lower-income New Yorkers had only led to economic ruin.[392] In late 1975, the mayor announced that rents would soon be raised by 8.5 percent on 180,000 apartments in the city, the beginning perhaps of the end of rent control that made living in New York possible for the less than wealthy. Tenant associations fought back, with the citywide rally held at Tudor City drawing local politicians who understood the importance of rent control despite the city's dire fiscal straights. State Senator Roy Goodman was there as usual, as was Bronx assemblyman John Dearie; the pair had worked together to help pass the Condominium and Cooperative Fair Practice Act that Governor Wilson had signed, as well the Emergency Tenants Protection Act, which limited the amount of rent that could be charged if a rent-controlled apartment were vacated and guaranteed new tenants a lease. While it was wonderful that some politicians were protecting the interests of middle- and lower-income New Yorkers, economic pressures would continue to make affordable housing in the city a major challenge for many for the foreseeable future.[393] Tudor City residents would have their own special set of challenges over the next decade and a half as their war with Harry Helmsley intensified.

Chapter 5

A UNIQUE PLACE, 1976–1989

Sometimes I think the only reason I stay in New York is because of this
pocket of sanity.
—Eileen Dasplin, resident of Tudor City, 1985

In the spring of 1989, visitors to two different art galleries in Manhattan—the Urban Center Gallery in midtown and the Bertha Urdang Gallery on the Upper East Side—had the opportunity to view the work of Israeli-born photographer Margalit Mannor. Mannor had spent four years taking photographs of Tudor City, sometimes sitting in her car for hours waiting for the light to hit the buildings in a certain way. Most people viewed the community as a nice place to live, but the artist perceived the beauty of what Fred French had created sixty years earlier in an uncommon way. "Sometimes I expect to see Cezanne or Picasso painting there," she said, thinking that the subject was every bit as picturesque and romantic as anything those two artists ever painted.[394]

The public display of Mannor's gorgeous photographs served as a happy, even fairytale-like ending to the story of Tudor City's first sixty years. Tudor City looked much the same as it did when Fred French had built it, but at the same time, the community had been transformed into something much different than what he had envisioned. New York City and the world of real estate were each rapidly changing in the late 1970s and 1980s as big money entered the game, pushing Tudor City, for better or worse, in a new direction. As forces contrary to the best interests of the residents of Tudor City intensified, so did the community's activist spirit, making this last chapter of the history of the city within a city a lesson in what ordinary people can do when united in a common and worthy pursuit. Through these years, Tudor City would be increasingly recognized as what someone who knew it best called "a unique place," with no other place on Earth quite like it.

SALUTE TO SPRING

What would turn out to be Tudor City's most eventful chapter in its history started out innocently enough. In May 1976, the building services employees in the complex went on strike, something they do now and then. (Indeed, the workers there are currently threatening to strike as I write this.) But like their Tudor City predecessors did during World War II, residents were jumping into the fray by volunteering to keep the place running. Some of the dozens of volunteers were acting as doormen and others as handymen, with yet others sorting mail and operating elevators. Sign-up sheets were posted in the buildings' lobbies, but it was understandably difficult to get people to work the graveyard shift. Because of that, some of the buildings' doors were locked from midnight to 6:30 a.m., meaning the only way to get in would be to call a tenant on the phone and have him or her open up. Tenants were tipping the volunteers with cookies and scotch, further bringing a small-town atmosphere to one of the biggest apartment complexes in New York City.[395]

The "Salute to Spring" Festival the community held that same month also brought a Norman Rockwell–like feeling to Tudor City. "Son of Sam" would in a few months terrorize the city, but no such fears could be detected at the old-fashioned block party that ran along Tudor City Place and the intersecting 41st, 42nd and 43rd Streets. Residents sold handmade artistic objects, most for five dollars or less, at more than one hundred small booths, this too perhaps something more likely to be found in a craft show in the country than in midtown Manhattan. The event recalled the popular tulip festivals of the late 1930s, when large crowds gathered in Tudor City's parks to celebrate the arrival of spring and revel in a strong sense of community uncommon in such an urban setting.[396]

This strong sense of community would soon prove to be a key asset as, once again, powerful forces threated the city within a city. After a few years of relative calm, Harry Helmsley, unhappy with the taxes he had to pay on the "vacant property" on which the two parks occupied, revived his attempt to turn the space into a revenue-generating asset. Helmsley admittedly viewed real estate as a game at which he was very good, with money the best means by which to keep score. The more money he made, the more he was winning the game, he figured, making financial gain his number-one priority regardless of the consequences to the tens of thousands of tenants in the hundreds of buildings he owned or co-owned. Additionally, Helmsley's second wife, who would prove to be every bit as tenacious as her husband, had very expensive tastes, more reason to do whatever it took to win the game.

In February 1979, frustrated by the opposition from tenants and local politicians he had faced soon after buying Tudor City when he said he would build on the parkland, Helmsley took an alternative tack. Seeing another property around the corner (that he likely viewed as "vacant" because it currently served as a city park), Helmsley proposed a swap: his fifteen thousand square feet of Tudor City parks for the ten-thousand-square-foot plot at the northwest corner of First Avenue and 43rd Street. Rather than put up two buildings on top of the Tudor City parks (one thirty stories and the other twenty-eight), he would erect one fifty-story tower, he stated, his glass structure to sit right behind Prospect Tower. No residents of that building had a river view anyway, he must have known, as Fred French did not want his renters to look out over (and smell) the slaughterhouses that stood there when he developed the area.[397]

Helmsley also must have known that all kinds of legal machinations would have to take place for the city to make such a deal. But that still seemed like the better alternative to having to again face John McKean and the elected officials who fully supported their constituencies in defending the parks should he exercise his "as of right" to build there. Rather than present his proposed tower as a luxury apartment building, Helmsley and his architectural firm (Emery Roth & Sons, which had designed the Pan Am Building) were careful to describe it in the media as an improvement for the neighborhood. The building would "significantly crystallize a modern boulevard personality for First Avenue by framing the United Nations in a cohesive and consistent fashion," as *New York Times* reporter Carter B. Horsley summarized the architects' portrayal of the tower (with just 375 apartments), a far more saleable proposition than an exclusive residence for wealthy people.[398]

Upon seeing the plans, however, local community groups and politicians concluded that Helmsley's proposed tower was something considerably less than an impressive architectural achievement that would improve the neighborhood. The fifty-story structure would make the UN's thirty-nine-story Secretariat Building look small, for one thing, reason enough to convince the city to turn down the proposed swap. More than that, however, the very idea of trading the privately owned parks for publically owned property was something that shouldn't even be considered, many felt, as doing so would encourage many developers to start bargaining for prime sites currently held by the city. Swapping city land for private use was a dangerous precedent, members of Community Board 6 (which held jurisdiction over the site) protested, with a variety of civic groups agreeing, including the Municipal Art Society, the Women's City Club and the Parks Council.[399]

With his plan to use the parks as leverage to get something even better foiled, Helmsley restated his intent to further develop Tudor City at the expense of its green space. It was now eight years after his initial attempt to expand the complex soon after buying it from the French Company, and he was more determined than ever to capitalize on his investment. Helmsley had won the long court battle to build over the Tudor City parks, and he and his lawyers wisely presented his plans as a simple exercising of his legal rights. In April 1979, however, speakers from the Tudor City Tenants Association rallied the community to try to stop this most recent threat, taking the stance that destroying two beautiful parks was a fundamentally wrong thing to do. The situation was serving as a prime example of what could happen when private and public interests collided and when environmental activism bumped into classic capitalism.[400]

Recognizing that the interests of many New Yorkers were at stake, city officials again stepped in to try to broker a deal in order to resolve the conflict. Rather than the failed "building density" deal in which Helmsley would have been awarded a bonus in how high and tall a structure he could put up on another property he owned in a different part of town, the developer was offered a forty-eight-thousand-square-foot city park at the southeast corner of First Avenue and 42nd Street as an alternative site for his proposed skyscraper. It was ex-mayor Robert Wagner, now chair of the New York City Planning Commission, who offered the deal to Helmsley in April, hoping that the developer would agree to the land swap to keep everybody happy. While the city's Planning Commission approved the swap, the deal required approval from the Board of Estimate.[401]

Interestingly, it appeared that Wagner and Gordon Davis, the city's parks commissioner, were not on the same page regarding this latest proposed land swap. Local kids and teens often could be found in what was considered the

United Nations Playground, Davis pointed out, with the head of parks clearly somewhat miffed that Wagner had not even consulted him about the proposed trade. Wagner was meeting with East Side legislators and community leaders on the matter, however, as the privatization of public parkland required a change in state law. Helmsley, meanwhile, was considering the alternative land swap but, at the same time, doing preliminary work at the Tudor City parks in preparation for excavation.[402]

A CHEAP SHOT

The 1980s began where the 1970s left off, with Helmsley still trying to replace the two parks with a modern tower. In May 1980, a team of sixteen construction workers attempted to put up a wooden fence around the north park over Memorial Day weekend, a sign that demolition was about to begin (bulldozers were also positioned nearby), but Helmsley's "sneak attack" (as one local politician called it) was promptly foiled when tenants removed the plywood panels. Police forced the protestors out of the park, allowing workers to start building the fence again, but Helmsley's crew was soon thwarted by more legal measures. Just an hour or so later, after the tenants were removed, Justice Martin Evans of the New York Supreme Court issued a restraining order to halt the erection of the (now nearly completed) fence and any excavation, with a hearing scheduled in a few days to hopefully settle the matter.[403]

Not surprisingly, it was John McKean who led the tenants' retaliation against the workers. Bullhorn in hand, McKean alerted fellow residents when he learned that Helmsley's squad had begun work, with appeals for them to stop unsuccessful. The next step was simply to remove their material, placing the wood on the sidewalks in a pass-along process à la water bucket brigade. "What a cheap shot," said Margaret Biesty, a ten-year resident of Tudor City, speaking of course of Helmsley's maneuver to begin work unannounced early in the morning on a holiday weekend. While the judge's stay was helpful, McKean knew that Helmsley was hardly done trying to build on the site. "This is only a breather and the war is not over," he remarked at the scene, an accurate prophecy. Making matters worse was that Helmsley's proposed buildings had nothing to do with the architecture, design or visual aesthetics of Tudor City. In its modern building completed in 1967, the Ford Foundation made a conscious and successful effort to "coordinate" with the architectural elements in the surrounding neighborhood, but no such attempt was being made with Helmsley's pair of skyscrapers to be set in the center of Tudor City itself.[404]

Meanwhile, Tudor City residents made it clear why the parks were so important to them. A half century and change after the first tenants moved in, residents still often referred to their community as a "city within a city," a kind of sanctuary from the storm that was most of Manhattan. "It is our oasis," another ten-year resident told a reporter, feeling—like almost all residents—that having two twenty-eight-story modern buildings plopped down in the middle of the community would take the heart and soul out of it. Indeed, while it was by no means perfect—the rent was going up, the buildings were old and required much upkeep, more unsavory characters were drifting into the neighborhood and the whole thing could be converted into a condominium or cooperative at any moment—Tudor City was for many as good as living in Manhattan could get circa 1980. A few days after the confrontation in the north park, some tenants used what was left of the wall to express their thoughts about the man who was trying to make Tudor City less of an oasis. "Why not be an angel and give us our parks?" one tenant had written, with another scribbling, "Only God can make a tree, don't take them away." A third simply read, "Creep," with no doubt who was the intended target.[405]

Happily, the young couples who had moved in about a decade earlier after the new rent-control law freed up apartments had produced a fair number of children, making Tudor City more family friendly. There was even now a Tudor City Junior Association, which arranged various activities for younger tenants. Kids could be found keeping their own mini-gardens, playing stickball, roller skating, biking and Easter egg rolling, and there was far less traffic in the area than most urban neighborhoods. Most of the children in Tudor City did not go to a country house on weekends or camp in the summer like their wealthier urban counterparts did, making the parks especially important as a play area. The parks, which were located at the geographic center of the complex, also served as a kind of commons where news was posted, and residents often gathered amid the maple, linden and magnolia trees to discuss issues relating to the community as a whole.[406]

Additionally, with its own post office, beauty parlor, supermarket and pub, Tudor City was still largely self-sufficient, just as French had intended it to be in 1925. The original stone floors, front desks, marble fireplaces and stained-glass windows remained, lending to the place a timeless quality. The tennis courts, ice skating rink and miniature golf course had fallen victim to development over the decades, but otherwise Tudor City looked and felt much like it did when the talkies first appeared in movie theaters. Given its character, quietness and the fact that rents were lower than comparable space in Midtown Manhattan (studios were now going for $260 to $340 and two-bedrooms for about $500), it was not surprising that Tudor City was 100 percent occupied and had a six-month waiting list to get in. Some

This "nook" in Windsor Tower is typical of the Tudor-style interiors that still exist in most of the buildings. *Wikimedia Commons (user Cc2723).*

The interior of this penthouse apartment in Windsor Tower likely looks much like it did when brand new some ninety years ago. *Wikimedia Commons (user Cc2723).*

apartments were rent-controlled and others rent-stabilized, with tenants of these units unlikely to leave as long as they were alive.[407]

Recognizing that Helmsley was not going to go away if the deal on the table didn't work out, the city's Planning Commission returned to its original idea of rezoning the parks as a means to save them. Attempting to avoid the unconstitutionality of the last rezoning nearly a decade ago, this proposal, drafted by a member of Community Board 6, would define a major development and any land next to it as a single building lot if each were commonly owned.[408] His ghost perhaps still haunting the place, Fred French had cleverly divided Tudor City into a handful of separate building lots so as not to exceed maximum density laws—a legal loophole that was coming into play more than a half century later.[409] The change in law would make it illegal to add any more buildings to Tudor City by making it clearer that the development had already had reached maximum construction density, something the author of the rezoning proposal and many other experts believed was already true.[410]

Despite all the potential snags and hitches, many of those directly or indirectly involved in the kerfuffle (but surely not Parks Commissioner Gordon Davis) hoped that Helmsley would take the large park offered by the city in exchange for the small two ones inside Tudor City. The *New York Times*, which followed the situation closely, urged each side to accept the terms in order to put an end to this ugly dispute that had already been going on much too long. While "far from an ideal solution," an editor wrote, it "appears to be the best realistic trade," exhorting Helmsley to take the site at 42nd Street and First Avenue and "add a very big new building to his collection, already the largest in New York, without destroying a fine feature of life in Tudor City."[411] The Tudor City Tenants Association was also attempting to have the community listed in the National Register of Historic Places in the hopes that simply being considered for such would at least delay Helmsley's plan. Approval of Tudor City's application for such status would by law stop Helmsley's bulldozers in their tracks, making that a smart way to buy some time until a possible deal could be made.[412]

State Senator Roy Goodman, who had served as a strong ally for Tudor City tenants from the very beginning of the battle for the parks, remained a voice of reason while Helmsley tumbled the numbers to determine if the trade was a fair one. There should be a six-month freeze on any activities related to the destruction of the Tudor City parks, he sensibly proposed at a meeting attended by city officials, with Helmsley's attorneys, and representatives of the Tudor City Tenant Association, perhaps thinking that a second confrontation between the developers' workers and angry tenants could turn violent. Such a freeze would offer enough time to work out the details of the trade that, based on the positive discussion at the meeting, appeared like Helmsley would accept.[413]

Indeed, just a few days later, the details of an agreement were released. Any demolition of the two parks would be delayed indefinitely until plans were completed and the agreement received court approval, the latter necessary because city and state property was involved. Helmsley had agreed to the swap of the parkland for the city-owned playground on which, if all went ahead as planned, a fifty-story apartment and office building would be constructed. The developer might have to replace the playground with another, the agreement specified, perhaps on a site along the East River and 34th and 35th Street that was currently a city-owned parking lot. The remnants of the wooden fence around the north park would be quickly removed, Goodman informed a group of happy tenants who had gathered at yet another rally, with hopefully this agreement to be the one that would stick. How much money the playground was worth, as determined by appraisers, was not yet clear, a detail that could potentially sink the deal because of state laws regarding property exchanges like this one.[414]

THE STORY OF DAVID AND GOLIATH

Not just the local newspapers but the national media recognized that the ruckus over Tudor City's parks made good copy as it continued to simmer over the next year. "You know the story of David and Goliath," wrote Ward Morehouse III in the *Christian Science Monitor*, likening the tale to the battle between the local residents, many of them old ladies living on their Social Security checks, and the real estate "kingpin." Some members of the tenant association, along with their kids and pets, had spent the night in the parks as a "sleep-in," riffing on the sit-ins that had been a popular form of protest activity in the late '60s. Residents took comfort in the fact that parks in different parts of the country—notably Park Place in Atlantic City, New Jersey; Overton Park in Memphis; and Jackson Park in Chicago—had been saved when citizens and government got involved. Those parks were public, however, making the fight for Tudor City's private parks a different and much more challenging test.[415]

Still, there was something going on in the country in the late 1970s and early 1980s when it came to parks, making it a good time for tenants to try to save the ones in Tudor City. "For many reasons people are now standing up for parks that are threatened with development," said Clint Page, a spokesman for the National League of Cities, thinking that the recent energy crisis created a greater awareness and appreciation of the environment. "There is an awful lot going on to save parks," agreed Mike Rogers of the United States Heritage Conservation and Recreation Service, especially so in New York City. Corporations like Avon were raising money to help improve Central Park, and Metropolitan Life Insurance Corporation and the New York Life Insurance Corporation were supporting the cleaning up of Madison Square Park (just blocks from Tudor City). Could a company with deep pockets perhaps rescue the Tudor City parks?[416]

Given Harry Helmsley's resolve to use the parks as a bargaining chip, the arrival of such an angel was highly unlikely. One might think that the deal made among the city, Helmsley and the Tudor City Tenants Association would be universally celebrated, but that was not the case. "New York City should not submit to threats by real estate interests and meekly hand over an East Side playground in a swap in order to prevent destruction of two small parks in the middle of the Tudor City development," wrote Philip K. Howard in a *New York Times* op-ed a few days after the agreement was announced. Howard was not a lawyer but rather the chairman of the planning and zoning committee of Community Board 6 who had just put forth the proposal to change the city's zoning law in order to deter developers from putting up skyscraper after skyscraper. Howard believed that Helmsley's so-called cheap trick was a cleverly designed strategy to get what he really wanted: the playground at First Avenue and 42nd Street. With an amazing view of the East River and the United Nations (as well as the Con Ed smokestacks), the proposed building did indeed seem superior (and likely more profitable) to whatever he could erect in Tudor City. As well, Helmsley had to be aware that taking away the Tudor City parks and squeezing two behemoths in the development would reduce the community's value, more reason to conclude that the man knew exactly what he was doing. Money, in short, was far more important to him than his public image.[417]

The deal that thus looked so good on paper to nearly everyone was for Howard a bad one. Losing the playground would be more than just an inconvenience for kids, as that district already ranked last in the city in that department. The presence of a fifty-foot tower would also steal some of the architectural thunder of the United Nations campus and, for much of the day, block the sun from shining on the thousands of windows on the Secretariat Building. "The ransom that Harry B. Helmsley demands is unacceptable," Howard concluded, imploring that "the city stand up to protect one of its scarcest resources."[418]

One person in particular, John McKean, was not happy to read Howard's op-ed piece. The president of the Tudor City Tenants Association scribbled off a letter to the editor of the *Times*, arguing that Howard had "misrepresented the facts completely." McKean had had lawyers for both the city and the association examine Howard's proposed amendment to the zoning laws, and they had concluded that this one, like the one put forth a decade ago, was unconstitutional. Besides that, McKean pointed out, Helmsley would have plenty of time to destroy the parks while the new law came into effect, making Howard's whole premise moot. McKean reiterated that the swap was the only realistic solution to the problem, thinking that using the courts to try to settle the matter would be, as it had been in 1972, a time-consuming, expensive and ultimately doomed path to take. "Our strength has been the force of public opinion and unity within the community," McKean wrote, convinced that the only way to defeat the most powerful real estate developer in the city (and perhaps the country) and save Tudor City's parks was to maintain a single voice.[419]

Despite McKean's call for unity, the back and forth between Community Board 6 and him continued. Now it was Joana Battaglia, chairperson of the board, who weighed in via her own letter to the editor to the newspaper. It was easy for McKean to recommend that the city give up a playground, she contended, as delivering that side of the bargain would cost Tudor City residents little or nothing any way one looked at it. Battaglia also felt that the amendment her colleague had proposed had a better chance of making it through the courts than McKean alleged, suggesting that independent counsel determine its constitutionality before concluding that it would be struck down. She went even further, however, suggesting that he and the common enemy might somehow be in cahoots. "There seems to be an unseemly confluence of Mr. McKean's position with that of Mr. Helmsley," Battaglia hinted not so subtly, insinuating that the two foes could be operating in a kind of alliance in order for each to get what he wanted out of the deal.[420]

Six months later, the land swap had still not come to a conclusion. In fact, the situation had become more complicated, as the very legality of the deal came into question. While Helmsley would have to squeeze his two buildings into Tudor City, the alternative site was a larger tract with a river view—by all appearances not a very fair trade. While an even swap might get through the courts, the fact that the city would be essentially losing money on the deal was likely to be deemed unlawful. Stein, Councilman Robert Dryfoos and Community Boards 6 and 7 made their opposition to the deal known to the City Planning Commission, as did, once again, the Municipal Art Society, the Women's City Club and the Parks Council. The East End Hockey Association also voiced its protest, not pleased that there would no longer be a place to play its sport (on roller skates on the cement "ice") should the playground disappear.[421]

Controversy continued to swirl around what *New York Times* architectural critic Paul Goldberger called "the complex drama." Other critics (including the New York chapter of the American Institute of Architects, which had originally supported the trade) were not happy to see how close Helmsley's fifty-story tower was to the Secretariat Building (225 feet, to be precise), a matter not just of aesthetics but security. As well, trading city property for private property remained a sticky issue, further casting the deal into real estate purgatory. The Parks Council was most vehemently opposed to the swap, not surprisingly, with the executive director of that organization going on the record to say that giving Helmsley what he wanted (or demanded, depending on your view) would represent "a surrender to blackmail." Tudor City tenants, meanwhile, remained hopeful that the deal would go through despite the ever-rising flak, with even the prospect of an enormous skyscraper going up in their backyard a better alternative than two smaller ones built over their parks. All parties were waiting to hear if the City Planning Commission would give its stamp of approval to the Board of Estimate, with that step to be taken in February 1981.[422]

While members of the commission calculated the pluses and minuses of the proposed deal, many New Yorkers observed the controversy with considerable interest. "For citizens concerned about issues of land use in New York," Goldberger wrote two weeks before the City Planning Commission decision would be announced, "this is as troubling a dispute as has been seen in years." While some viewed the outcome, if indeed consummated, as a win-win given that each principal player would get what it wanted, others saw the identical result as a lose-lose. Either a city park and frequently used playground or the "crown jewels" of Tudor City would be lost, a more cynical spectator could reasonably conclude, making the whole affair a sad one in the city's recent history. Helmsley had already offered the city an additional $1 million to create another recreational facility nearby, a clear indication that he would be delighted to add the new tower to his portfolio if awarded the opportunity.[423] As an extra incentive for the City Planning Commission to approve the swap, Helmsley agreed to reduce the height of his tower to forty-six stories so that it would be only somewhat higher than the thirty-nine-story Secretariat Building across 42nd Street.[424]

Right on schedule, the City Planning Commission announced its decision: Helmsley would be permitted to trade the Tudor City parkland (which was legally considered a vacant building lot) for the city playground at First Avenue and 42nd Street, contingent, of course, on approval by the Board of Estimate. That group had sixty days to vote yay or nay, with some opposition to the swap expected. The City Planning Commission admitted that, despite its vote, the deal was not ideal. "We felt there was no happy answer," said Herbert J. Sturz, chairperson of the commission, concluding that it was the only feasible way to maintain the character of Tudor City. A majority vote of three-quarters by the Board of Estimate was now required, however, a hurdle that even Sturz believed would prove too high for the trade to actually take place.[425]

Oddly, editors of the *New York Times* considered the exchange a done deal, even though the Board of Estimate had yet to vote on the issue. The city had learned a valuable lesson with what the newspaper called the "Tudor Deal," counting chickens before they hatched. Tudor City's parks had been originally mapped out as separate zoning lots, the editors correctly pointed out, making them fair game for development for whoever owned them. "Unless the city takes the lesson to heart, the same thing could happen again," the newspaper warned, recommending that other residential areas with parks or open spaces like Stuyvesant Town, Peter Cooper Village and Ruppert House in Manhattan; Parkchester in the Bronx; and Fresh Meadows in Queens be promptly designated as Special Planned Community Preservation Districts to avoid having to take another bad deal with a landlord.[426]

Andrew Stein, Manhattan Borough president, was, however, quick to warn that the "Tudor Deal" was by no means a deal yet. In a letter to the editor published a week after the latest editorial in that newspaper about Tudor City, Stein reminded readers that the Board of Estimate still had to approve the proposed trade and that that group approached such matters from a different perspective. "The board is the lawful caretaker of the public trust and must protect the public interest," he made clear, insinuating that the giving away of a city park and playground to a private developer was the kind of thing that these officials were likely to frown on. Such a deal, if made, could very well set a precedent, as Community Board 6 had argued, potentially triggering a wholesale trading of public land to private interests across the five boroughs. "We must not allow public parks to be offered as ransom to developers who threaten privately owned properties and hold them hostage," Stein stated, a voice of reason in what was by all measures a difficult situation to neatly resolve.[427]

An Essential Service

While strongly opposing the land swap, Stein was hardly willing to allow Helmsley to, as he put it, "destroy Tudor City." Before he became president of the borough, Stein had served nine years as state assemblyman in Tudor City's district, making him intimately familiar with the value of the parks to residents. There were other options to save those parks, he believed, leaning toward the kind of zoning changes that Community Board 6 had recommended but that the City Planning Commission had dismissed. In short, the deal the Board of Estimate was considering was a bad one for the city, Stein argued, thinking that the site Helmsley would receive was worth at least $30 million more than the financial value of the Tudor City parks property.[428]

Even before the official decision by the Board of Estimate, it was becoming clear that the deal would be squashed. It was Ed Koch, now mayor of the city, who was leading the opposition to the swap, a revelation given his support for the Tudor City Tenant Association during his representative days. Koch had originally supported the exchange, likely seeing it as the best way to save the parks, but in March 1981, he reversed his position, unwilling to bow to Helmsley's demands.[429] In addition to Koch and Stein, City Council president Carol Bellamy was leaning toward opposition, making the prospect of approval a long shot at best. (The deal would require nine out of eleven votes, with Bellamy alone having two of them.) With the trade seemingly off, what would Harry Helmsley do, many wondered, the man's reputation for not giving up easily very well deserved.[430]

Indeed, less than a week after the disclosure that the Board of Estimate would kill the deal, Helmsley, or rather his attorneys, went into action. The owners of Tudor City "intend to exercise their rights," tenants were informed, with building on the parks planned to start after the requisite fifteen-day notice. City officials were now scrambling to find yet another piece of property on which Helmsley could put up a new tower, hoping that a different deal could be made to stop the destruction of the parks.[431] While that scenario played out, the city also decided to put its own team of lawyers on the case. The Housing and Preservation Committee quickly filed suit in New York Supreme Court to stop Helmsley from building on the parkland, something that was perhaps inevitable based on the inability for all parties to come to terms without litigation. It was illegal for a landlord to take away "an essential service," the suit asserted, meaning that Tudor City tenants were entitled to continue to use the parks simply because that was part of why they were paying rent.[432]

While the legal wheels spun on that front, the effort to find another site for Helmsley continued for the next few months. Helmsley's attorneys had given the city "a reasonable amount of time" to look for a property before beginning work in the Tudor City parks, but the developer and his lawyers were beginning to lose patience.[433] The city did indeed find such a site, one just nine blocks north on First Avenue. The Board of Estimate agreed to appraise the property in hopes that this land for land trade would resolve the seemingly endless dispute over the Tudor City parks.[434] There was no park or playground involved, nor would a tower be within a stone's throw of the UN's Secretariat Building, making some feel this could be the one that would be the best option (or at least the least bad one).

Again, however, there was a catch. No fewer than three appraisers for the property, located at 51st Street, valued it as significantly less than what the city believed it was worth, making it impossible to offer that site to Helmsley as an even swap for the Tudor City parks. A number of developers had offered more than $12 million for the property (on which a four-story, eighty-year-old building currently stood), making it smarter for the city to sell and take the cash rather than give to Helmsley. The city wanted to avoid what had happened with the proposed city playground swap, when a certain real estate developer offered his take on the deal. It was then that Helmsley's rival in real estate, Donald J. Trump, announced that the playground was worth significantly more than Tudor City's parks, something that had contributed to the Board of Estimate's backing out of the deal.[435] (Trump had joined his father's real estate company in 1968 and was currently developing Trump Tower.) Andrew Stein had actually invited Trump into the process, with the future president making an offer for the playground that was significantly more than its appraised value.[436]

Again no deal would take place, however, when in January 1982 Mayor Koch decided that giving the 51st Street property to Helmsley as compensation for the Tudor City parks was "fiscally unsound."[437] And need it be said, the community's parks were again in peril, as Helmsley reintroduced his plan to erect two buildings on the site. The man also planned to sue the city for $40 million to $50 million in damages, a response to what he believed was a concerted effort on the part of local officials to block the development of the "vacant lot" for almost a dozen years now. The New York Supreme Court case filed by the Tudor City Tenants Association arguing that the parks were "an essential service" was still pending, however, meaning that Helmsley could not yet legally begin construction.[438] Would this situation ever be resolved, one had to wonder?

It would, of course, but not before Harry Helmsley seized an opportunity to make life more difficult for Tudor City residents. In May 1983, the landlord sent a New York City legal form (Demand Form AMO-1A) to every tenant demanding the names of everyone who was living in his or her apartment. Although his lawyers denied it, Helmsley was taking advantage of a new law stating that occupants who were not family members of the person(s) who leased the apartment could potentially be evicted (presumably because of the danger of overcrowding). Many residents, especially older people, understandably found the forms, which were sent by registered mail and required a notarized response, intimidating and frightening, thinking that they or a roommate might be evicted. McKean was deluged with phone calls from concerned tenants, and ally Carol Bellamy and Anthony B. Gliedman, the city's commissioner of Housing Preservation and Development, immediately filed a suit to have the mailings stopped. This was yet another attempt by Helmsley to try to get rid of tenants in rent-controlled and rent-stabilized apartments, as doing such would allow the landlord to charge twice the rent with a new lease.[439] A spokesman for Helmsley shifted the blame, however, claiming that the forms were sent only after bona fide tenants complained about strangers living in some apartments. The tenants considered these people to be a security problem, this story went, accusing them also of stealing their mail.[440]

While the incident was no joking matter to residents worrying that they or their roommate could soon be out on the street, Sydney H. Schanberg of the *New York Times* found Helmsley's latest scheme ripe for sarcasm. Tudor City had always been and remained one of the safest and most staid neighborhoods in Manhattan, but the landlord was presenting the community as a scary and dangerous place in order to defend the mass mailing of Demand Form AMO-1A. "Are the legions of Darth Vader taking over?" Schanberg quipped (Episode VI of the *Star Wars* franchise, *Return of the Jedi*, had just been released), jesting that Helmsley had sent the form to learn "who was slipping into his eight buildings and whether Luke

Skywalker and his Jedi had to be called in to smite the evil forces." Like residents, however, city officials did not find the man's use of the form at all amusing, charging him with "an abuse of process and a nuisance" and issuing a restraining order against his continued use of it.[441]

The battle over the two Tudor City parks had been raging since Richard Nixon was president, but by July 1983, it appeared that the end was in sight. It was then that the City Rent Control Office denied Helmsley permission to build apartment towers on the contested site, basing its decision on the courts' recent ruling that the parks were indeed "an essential service" for tenants (only those with rent-controlled apartments, another reason why the man was so eager to see them go). Again Helmsley's lawyers made it known that they would appeal to the New York Supreme Court, claiming that the ruling was "blatantly unconstitutional." The fact that the developer would not only not be able to build on his own land but also receive zero compensation must have rankled the man who usually got his way, one way or another. The tide was now clearly turning against Helmsley, however, as more elected officials, under pressure from their respective constituencies, did what they could to make the city a more livable place. The fiscal crisis of the 1970s and its politics of austerity were gone, replaced in the early 1980s by a new kind of effort to protect and preserve what could never be replaced.[442]

A little more than a year later, Helmsley would lose not just one appeal but two, with one witness telling the city's Conciliation and Appeals Board that the parks were for the enclave "a communal back yard."[443] Even before that ruling, however, the now seventy-four-year-old Helmsley was seeing the writing on the wall and soon announced that he was exiting the rental market completely and putting Tudor City up for sale. Rental housing was "an impossible business to be in," he had decided, with his thirteen-year experience owning the complex no doubt contributing to that conclusion. The developer was already in the process of selling some of his eight buildings, with Times Equities Inc., a company with experience converting rental apartments to cooperatives, eager to buy them. Helmsley could have tried to convert the buildings himself, but the man said that he had his hands full doing just that at two of his other properties: Parkchester in the Bronx and Park West Village (on Central Park West north of 97th Street). Conversion from rentals to ownership often took years, and one would think that Helmsley already had had more than enough of Tudor City.[444]

We Like It the Way It Is

Helmsley was not completely done with Tudor City, however. Along with a few partners, the developer was soon trying to convert one of the buildings he still owned, the Manor, into a co-op. His old nemesis, John McKean, was at it again, this time blocking the conversion because it was not fully clear whether potential purchasers (or even future renters) of the apartments would have access to the parks. "The plan fails to disclose whether purchasers and nonpurchasing tenants will have the right to continued use of the existing private parks," the State Attorney General's Office noted in September 1984, giving Helmsley's group forty-five days to file an amended plan. Tenants in 2 Tudor City Place (what had been called Tudor City Gardens) were watching this latest fight with considerable interest, as that building was the next one to be converted. "In Tudor City, such acrimony has become normal," Kirk Johnson wrote in the *New York Times* in reporting the story, with readers likely wondering what it was about that particular community that made it such a battleground.[445]

This battle with McKean and the city would prove to be the last for Helmsley and his partners at Tudor City. "We're fed up with the punishment the tenants are giving us and the city, too," explained Alvin Schwartz, one of Helmsley's partners, in May 1985, likely thinking that the pickings would be better elsewhere. "They are not parks," Schwartz added, defining the green spaces the tenants had fought so hard to preserve as "two lots we've been paying taxes on since year one." The buyers of their remaining properties (six of the buildings as well as the four brownstones and parkland) were Philip Pilevsky of Philips International and Francis Greenburger of Time Equities, who were planning to convert the buildings to cooperatives. (The pair was already involved with the conversion of four other buildings in the community.) The parks would be donated to a public trust, a good (but not guaranteed) strategy of avoiding the real estate taxes to which Schwartz referred.[446]

It appeared that Tudor City's parks were out of the woods, so to speak, regarding future threats from Harry Helmsley, but there was always the possibility that the new owners could similarly determine they were "two lots" on which to build. Gaining landmark status, something that had been explored for more than a decade now, remained the best way for Tudor City to protect itself from real estate moguls like Helmsley (and the city itself) from both new construction and modern modifications that would alter the character of the community. In December 1985—almost fourteen years after John McKean first approached the Landmarks Preservation Commission—tenants had the opportunity to tell the group why they believed it should receive the status. "We like it the way it is," McKean explained as to why he and dozens of other tenants were pursuing the designation, adding that "it's a unique place." All exterior alterations would have to be approved if the complex was designated a historic district, but McKean felt it was well worth it. The commission had already determined that Tudor City was a "pioneering venture in private urban renewal," a positive sign. Still, the pro-landmark contingent was not taking any chances, planning to bring maps, models and slides to the meeting with the commission to make its point. One man was considering arriving in medieval dress to further illustrate the "Tudorness" of Tudor City, a throwback perhaps to the costumed "knaves" who would sing Christmas carols as part of the annual burning of the Yule Log.[447]

While at just nineteen buildings (the twelve original buildings, four brownstones, Church of the Covenant and two other apartment buildings) and parks, the landmarked district would be quite small compared to some others (Greenwich Village encompassed some two thousand buildings), but Tudor City had much of what members of the commission liked to see. Early examples of garden city planning were increasingly being recognized

331 East 41st Street, one of the few buildings in the area to have survived the development of Tudor City, adjacent to the park. *Photo by Piero Ribelli.*

336–340 East 43rd Street. This row of three brownstones also skirted Fred French's wrecking ball. *Photo by Piero Ribelli.*

as being ahead of their time as the pedestrian-friendly "new urbanism" movement gained traction. Many of the amenities were long gone (one can only shudder about what Helmsley would have thought about the indoor or outdoor golf courses), but some residents no doubt walked to work in the midtown business district just as Fred French had planned sixty years earlier. Indeed, while acrimony had ruled since Helmsley bought the place in 1971, the community had hardly changed in terms of both its architecture and the people drawn to it. "It's a great and beautiful middle-class enclave that should be preserved and protected," said Gary Papush, a member of local Community Board 6, his testimony like that of his colleagues likely to carry significant weight at the December meeting.[448]

True to their word, the new buyers of Tudor City were pledging in their co-op offering to set up a not-for-profit corporation that would ensure that the parks remain parks. Owners of apartments in the Manor, the first building to go co-op, would have "continued access to the two Tudor City parks," the prospectus stated, good news as the other buildings gradually converted from rentals. Time Equities and Philips International were also kicking in $100,000 to the trust with the estimated 10 percent interest to go to expenses and upkeep, something Helmsley likely would have scoffed at. (He had fired the full-time gardener as soon as he purchased Tudor City.) Most of the tenants wanted their parks to remain private, but that was wishful thinking given the tax perk the owners would receive by making them public. Still, it was believed that Time Equities and Philips International would make about $100 million by converting seven buildings in Tudor City, a fair piece of change in 1986.[449]

Along with the conversion to a cooperative, the official awarding of the two parks to the community marked a new era for Tudor City. In May 1987, Tudor City Greens, a nonprofit group of tenant representatives, took title to the parks, ending a fifteen-year battle with the previous owner. While that group owned the property, a national organization called the Trust for Public Land owned the development rights that could never be sold or transferred. And because of a conservation property right, the fifteen thousand square feet of space would forever be a park, a happy ending to what was an ugly chapter in the history of Tudor City and New York City real estate. Also good news was that Time Equities and Philips International bumped up their contributions to the trust to $800,000 for maintaining and upgrading the parks, placating some residents who felt its initial offer of $100,000 was insufficient given how much profit would be realized.[450]

The parks victory deservedly made John McKean a hero within the community. Older women, a group that most frequently could be found in the two parks, were especially grateful for the man's relentless effort to save the space and for his courage to tangle with one of the wealthiest and most powerful individuals in the country. He had also taken on the largest foundation in the nation when it showed signs of possibly encroaching on Tudor City, casting the tenant association as a David prepared to do battle with any Goliath that presented a threat to the community. McKean, now seventy-nine years old, had planned to manage his portfolio, read a lot of books and go fishing after he retired from Fish and Mavin, the real estate company where he had been president. But fate stepped in when the parks were put in jeopardy back in 1971, a fortunate thing for residents past and present and for the city as a whole.[451]

With the parks matter finally settled and the development transitioning to cooperatives, McKean would have more time to catch bluefish off the coast of Nantucket as he had planned. Newly formed co-op boards would take away much of the power he had wielded as head of the tenant association, although McKean would hold a seat on the new parks group, Tudor City Greens, and would continue to represent those residents who chose not to buy their apartments. Not surprisingly, McKean was staying put in Tudor

Tudor City Greens manages the development's now public parks. *Photo by Piero Ribelli*.

City; he and his wife, Betty, had just purchased both of the apartments they had been renting in the Manor. And until Tudor City Greens took over maintenance of the parks, it was business as usual, the first thing being the annual cleanup of the green space. Fifty residents would soon descend on the parks, gardening implements literally in hand.[452]

While the Landmark Preservation Commission considered its decision, quite a few apartments in the Manor were beginning to sell, much in part due to the "insider prices" that were being offered to the building's tenants as an incentive for a limited period of time. Given the sizable discount that could be had for renters who were able to scrape up the down payment, buying now was a smart investment. Residents were given the opportunity to purchase a one-bedroom apartment for about $80,000 to $100,000 and a two-bedroom for $100,000 to $150,000, while outsiders would have to pay about twice that.[453] Inside sales in two buildings (Prospect Tower and the Cloister) that were converting to co-ops were initially slow, however, as many residents, especially older ones on fixed incomes in rent-controlled or rent-stabilized apartments, either didn't have the cash or didn't want to own property at this point in their lives. As well, some of the buildings were in rough shape and needed significant work, which meant high maintenance fees, another legacy of Helmsley's disastrous tenure as owner. The initial slow insider sales incentivized Time Equities to advertising the offerings in the *New York Times*, *New York* magazine and the *Village Voice*, which did the trick, even at the outsider prices.[454]

A SENSE OF PLACE

The conversion of Tudor City from rentals to cooperatives dovetailed nicely with the effort to have the community declared a historic district by the city's Landmark Preservation Committee. That effort had begun in the 1970s as one of the potential avenues through which the tenant association could save its parks from Helmsley's wrecking ball. The parks had been saved by new ownership and via the trust that had been created, but McKean and others continued to pursue the historic designation through the 1980s in order to further protect the community from future development. The December 1985 public hearing with the committee had been a positive one (thirty people spoke in favor of the designation), but many more steps had to be taken for Tudor City to be awarded the prized status.[455]

Indeed, Tudor City was just one of many districts in the city hoping to receive further consideration from the Landmarks Preservation Committee in the late 1980s. Activists believed that the committee moved at a snail-like pace and were concerned that developers could knock down buildings that should be saved while the long process continued. Developers meanwhile, were convinced that the committee wielded too much power and was "anti-progress," making the issue of preservation a highly contested site in New York City. Because it was relatively small, highly self-contained and, for the most part, architecturally coherent, Tudor City had an advantage over larger districts with buildings of different eras and styles. Still, gaining the status was by no means guaranteed, reason enough for more activist residents to continue to push the committee to make its decision.[456]

It can be understood why the Landmarks Preservation Committee took its time in determining the fate of districts or buildings in the city. In the two decades following 1965, the year it was created, the committee had declared forty-eight districts as historic, with a handful more currently under consideration. In August 1986, the group was reviewing a developer's proposal to put up a high-rise building in the South Street Seaport area and a six-story structure in Greenwich Village, a good example of the range of projects it had to evaluate. In almost all cases, a group of concerned citizens made its presence known, hoping that the commission would decide to preserve the character of its respective neighborhood by blocking plans for a new building or modification. The phrase "a sense of place" could often be heard in the meetings, as activists argued that a stable physical landscape was essential to maintaining the identity of a particular community. Residents of Tudor City had emphasized this point in the most recent session with the committee, seeing the faux medieval village that Fred French had created in the 1920s as not just architecturally important or unique but an environment that heavily defined and informed who they were as individuals and as a community.[457]

With such a passion, it was not surprising that activists were frustrated by the Landmarks Preservation Commission's deliberate and methodical ways. A historic district had not been declared since 1981, when the Upper East Side was awarded that status. Besides having a slim staff and budget constraints, the commission had to take into account legal standards and historical context for any district or building under consideration, making the endeavor a highly complex and emotionally charged process. In Manhattan alone, nervous residents or friends of not just Tudor City but the Upper West Side, West Village, Tribeca, Murray Hill and the Ladies Mile (an expanse of nineteenth-century department stores near Union Square) were wondering why the commission was not treating their neighborhood as the number-one priority. Developers, meanwhile, were exasperated not just by the pace of the commission but by its legal right to declare a whole part of town as a historic district and, by doing so, thwart what they termed "revitalization." Property owners also had to go before the group for putting in new windows or altering the entry of an old building, making them also think that the commission had far too much sway in determining the architectural landscape of New York City.[458]

By early 1988, there were signs that, after years of waiting patiently in queue, Tudor City was becoming the landmark commission's top priority. Renowned architect Robert A.M. Stern had written a letter to the commission in support of Tudor City (one of many sent to the commission) that, in praising the architectural value of the community, made more people aware of its existence. "With its fine…detailing, Tudor City rises above the park like a magnified English country home," he wrote, thinking that the development "gives to the public more than it takes: open space, light, a magnificent frame for the axis of Forty-Second Street, and a sense of place." Such letters of support from acknowledged experts carried significant weight with the commission and vastly improved the chances of the district receiving historic status.[459]

Winter scene in the parks. *Wikimedia Commons (April Anderson)*.

The Tudor City Association ("Tenant" had been dropped with the conversion to cooperatives) was also actively bringing greater public awareness of the community as a means to improve the chances of its being named a historic district. The association's Historic Preservation Committee had recently put on a "Historic Tudor City Day," which took visitors back to medieval times in order to highlight its architectural value. The public was invited to take guided tours of the community led by a man dressed as a beefeater (the guards of the British Royal Palace and Tower of London). While sipping on hot cider and snacking on sweetmeats, visitors to Tudor City, many of them seeing the place for the first time, viewed a slide show featuring the ornamental details of the buildings. Medieval-era music added to the experience in which guests learned about Tudor-style architecture and the history of the Tudor family following its victory of the War of the Roses. The parks in different seasons were also highlighted in the slide show, with the committee fully aware that the beauty of the snow-covered split-rail fence in the winter and the maple trees blooming in the spring would move visitors.[460]

Those roaming about Tudor City and taking in the pointed archways, checkerboard brickwork and rosettes were also informed that Tudor City Greens had recently hired landscape architect Lee Weintraub to restore the parks to their original design. This was one more way the association's Historic Preservation Committee was attempting to sway members of the city's Landmark Preservation Commission to award the district historic designation. While Tudor City looked much like it did in the late 1920s, when the original buildings were being completed, some changes had naturally taken place over the past sixty years. Some residents who had lived in the community for decades not so fondly recalled when it overlooked the slaughterhouse district, with vivid memories of the animals being led to their killing and the smell that drifted west on windier days. None of the modern towers that now heavily populated the neighborhood was around in these pre-UN days, and a resident looking west from a high floor in one of the Tudor City buildings could not only see the New York Public Library on Fifth Avenue but also the Jersey shore. Irrespective of its architectural attributes, Tudor City was without question "historic," one could argue, a remnant of a mostly lost and continually disappearing period of New York City.[461]

Visitors to Tudor City learn a bit of its storied history via plaques on the gate to the park. *Photo by Piero Ribelli.*

Tudor City proudly declares its status as a historic district. *Photo by Piero Ribelli.*

A Medieval Fantasy

The ongoing conversion of Tudor City from rentals to cooperatives and the growing sense that a decision from the Landmarks Preservation Committee was forthcoming raised the public profile of the apartment complex. The amazing history of the development was now frequently being told in the media, especially its revolutionary beginnings in the 1920s and its tumultuous chapter while under the ownership of Harry Helmsley in the 1970s and early 1980s. While it had been around since Charles Lindbergh flew solo across the Atlantic, it was apparent that many people were just discovering the existence of Tudor City. Even many longtime New Yorkers had never seen it, having had no reason to venture that far east in midtown, and journalists, too, seemed to be encountering it for the first time. Beth Sherman of *Newsday*, for example, described the community in early 1988 as one that "sports the symbols of a bygone English era," clearly taken with the, well, Tudorness of the place:

> *A medieval fantasy of Gothic arches, gargoyles and coats of arms unfolds on a 5 ½-acre bluff....Limestone unicorns and griffins rise from turrets, like oversized chess pieces. Tapestry rugs and dark throne-like chairs decorate lobbies. A knight in shining armor adorns a hand-painted stained-glass window that glows blood red in the early morning light. Two pristine parks in the middle of the complex serve as a modern-day village green.*[462]

On May 17, 1988, Tudor City received its prized landmark status, making it officially a historic district (the fifty-second in New York City). Tudor City was "an early and eminently successful attempt to implement the principles of Garden City planning in a high-density urban environment," the commission's report stated, with members voting unanimously (8–0) that the buildings, parks and playgrounds included in the district should be so protected. "Tudor City is much more than an assemblage of significant buildings in a 'medieval' style," the report noted, recognizing the development as "a highly successful attempt to urbanize that style."[463] Not surprisingly, members of Tudor City's Historic Preservation Committee were overjoyed, as were most of its seven thousand residents, in knowing that the place would remain just as it was, its uniqueness preserved.[464] (Owners of the Hotel Tudor, aware that no alterations could be made to the building without permission of the landmarks commission, had objected to its designation.) Some residents had begun to replace the

This rooftop of a penthouse apartment in Windsor Tower seems to be from another time and place against the contemporary Manhattan skyline. *Wikimedia Commons (user Cc2723).*

original multiple-pane casement windows with standard double-hung sash windows, an alteration that would soon no longer be allowed.[465]

It was clear from the commission's designation report that the eight members fully appreciated the historical importance of Tudor City to the city. "The significance of Tudor City to the architectural history of New York is multifaceted," a paragraph in the summary began, with the commission agreeing:

> *It stands as the well-conceived descendant and culmination of the "communal" complexes which began, in New York, with such projects as the Home Buildings in Cobble Hill. Tudor City insured the return to middle-class respectability of midtown's East Side, which had begun with Sutton Place and Beekman Terrace. Similarly, Tudor City became the most extravagant example of Tudor Revival architecture—a tradition which moved during the early twentieth century from suburban mansions to urban apartment buildings. The complex is a premier example of an architectural design sensitive to its physical context (through its siting and detailing) and to its complex program (through the integration of services with "efficiency" apartments).[466]*

Architectural detail (bird). *Photo by Piero Ribelli.*

Architectural detail (boar). *Photo by Piero Ribelli.*

Architectural detail (crown). *Photo by Piero Ribelli.*

While the original buildings themselves—constructed out of red brick with ornamentation of limestone, sandstone and/or terra cotta on their tops and bottoms—were admittedly not all that interesting, the embellishments were and thus were instrumental in putting over the top.[467]

As anyone who has visited Tudor City and looked up could tell you, the heraldic designs on the buildings are indeed nothing less than extraordinary. It would have been faster and cheaper to cut corners, but Fred French and his team spent considerable time and money borrowing from the Tudor and Elizabethan architectural vernacular. A shield of Henry VII (the first of the Tudor kings) can be found on the respective roofs of Prospect, Tudor and Windsor Towers, for example, while a swan, German shield and stag's head are a few of the ornamentations of Essex House. A falcon and portcullis adorn the Manor, while a boar's head, griffins, ships, a fleur-de-lis, Norman shields, ermines and, fittingly, Tudor roses add to the beauty of Tudor Tower. If one squints one's eyes a bit, the buildings' heraldic designs make the visitor feel as if he or she is in another time or place than twenty-first-century New York City, one reason why the committee designated Tudor City as a historic district.[468]

Visitors to the Bertha Urdang Gallery about one year after Tudor City was awarded historic designation might have concluded the same.

Architectural detail (gargoyle). *Photo by Piero Ribelli.*

Architectural detail (griffin). *Photo by Piero Ribelli.*

Architectural detail (ram). *Photo by Piero Ribelli*

Margalit Mannor's large, colorful photographs of Tudor City on the walls of the gallery were contemporary yet revealed the timelessness of the place, bringing back strong memories for those who had once lived there. "This was the real New York," observed Kent Barwick of the Municipal Art Society in his introduction to the show's catalogue, remembering Tudor City in the early 1960s as a "lofty fortress guarded by doormen" that "seemed to be at the very center of things." In her own piece for the catalogue, Barbara Head Millstein of the Brooklyn Museum recalled Tudor City as "a kind of Camelot, a golden castle at twilight" when she visited the place as a teenager in the late 1940s. Tudor City remains a kind of Camelot, I think, a legendary and mythical place that is, at the same time, entirely and unquestionably real.[469]

EPILOGUE

*It's across from the United Nations in one of the busiest corners of Manhattan, yet
Tudor City remains obscure and mysterious to those who live beyond its borders.*
—Beth Stebner, New York Daily News, *2014*

A lthough it's safe to say that most Americans have probably never heard of
the place, the history of Tudor City is a truly remarkable one. Consider
the story as an extended elevator pitch that might go something like this:

*Fred Fillmore French, New York City's real estate "boy wonder," goes from
rags to riches to build the largest residential complex in the city to that point
in time. After completing one of the earliest examples of urban renewal in
the country in the Roaring Twenties, French uses the financing plan he had
invented to raise millions of dollars in a short period of time. The complex,
whose architecture recalled that of sixteenth-century England, is an immediate
success, but the Great Depression brings his company to the brink of financial
ruin. Suddenly, French dies at age fifty-two, not living to see the heyday of his
development during World War II and the postwar years due to the economic
boom and housing shortage. The United Nations decides to move next door,
causing considerable friction, but that is nothing compared to the tumult that
takes place a few decades later when the most powerful real estate developer in
the city buys the complex. This man (the archrival of the future president of
the United States, who makes a brief appearance in the story) tries to destroy
the community's village green, but a hero emerges who saves the day.*

While this highly condensed, only slightly inflated history of Tudor City ends thirty years ago, the community lived on of course. Comparatively speaking, however, the last three decades have been relatively tranquil ones for Tudor City, good news after the *sturm und drang* of the 1970s and 1980s. Much of the news surrounding the community in recent years has involved the need to abide by the regulations imposed by the Landmarks Preservation Commission in awarding the district historic status. The designation has proved to a mixed blessing of sorts; while landmark status has indeed protected the neighborhood from further development, it has also made any alteration to the buildings impossible without permission from the commission (just as intended). Adding a casement air conditioner is not allowed because it would detract from the original façade, for example, something dozens of residents learned firsthand when their units were rather abruptly removed by a co-op board in 2007.[470] Preserving the original façade has also turned out to be a major expense for many of the buildings, as the ninety-year-old terra cotta has a tendency to crumble or break off and fall to the ground. Costly lawsuits have resulted when people were struck by the ornamentation, and the city's Department of Buildings has ratcheted up its inspections to ensure that the buildings' exteriors are safe.

While coming home to find your air conditioner gone was an inconvenience to say the least, protecting sightlines and environmental conditions in the community has been the most politically charged activity of residents in recent years. Although no new buildings can be added to the complex, they can be in the surrounding area, something that could have an effect on the quality of life for Tudor City residents. In 2008, for example, residents sued the City Council and City Planning Commission to block the construction of what would be one of Manhattan's largest development projects. Seven new towers along the East River (on the former Con Ed site) would bring darkness and dirt to the "urban Eden" that was Tudor City, as *AM New York* described the community, forcing residents to once again protect their enclave.[471] Rumors are today again swirling about the construction of new buildings along the river, suggesting that not much has changed in the neighborhood over the past fifty years.

Naturally, so to speak, the two parks that residents fought so hard to keep remain the centerpiece of the community. In 1994, Tudor City Greens hired landscape architect Nina J. Kramer to reconstruct the parks, which were described that year by Christopher Gray of the *New York Times* as "a bit ragged but still delightful." The parks would become better lit, for one thing, and the gravel paths rearranged for a better flow. But besides those changes, some additional shrubs and a new iron fence that closely matched the original one, the parks would look much the same as they did almost a half century earlier when Robert Moses came along to take a twenty-two-foot swath to improve the approach to the United Nations.[472]

While the UN and Tudor City have been generally good neighbors since the world organization settled on Turtle Bay as its permanent home, there has been the occasional row. In 1994, residents complained about the noise coming across First Avenue from groups protesting one thing or another at Ralph Bunche Park, Hammarskjold Plaza or 42nd Street. (Rallies were not allowed on the sidewalk in front of the UN for security reasons.) "The demonstrations are like rock concerts in our living rooms," griped Harry Laughlin, the president of the Tudor City Association who had replaced John McKean when he died in February 1993 at eighty-five years old.[473] To make matters worse, the protests were often held on evenings and weekends, as that was when people had the time to devote to their respective causes—this despite the fact that the UN offices were closed then. Laughlin had measured the noise level at 112 decibels, a function of loudspeakers and amplified megaphones that the Founding Fathers could not have anticipated when they made free speech a fundamental right of Americans. The association was urging the city to restrict where, when and how loud the protests could be, in some way echoing the campaign against Con Ed decades ago for its own audible and environmental pollution.[474]

The following year, it was part of Tudor City itself that was getting on some residents' nerves. The co-op board at Prospect Tower (now simply referred to as 45 Tudor City Place) was seeking to ditch the giant "Tudor City" sign on its roof, telling the Landmarks Preservation Commission that the once brightly lit advertisement for the community (easily seen from Times Square) was now just a worthless pile of scrap metal. (Another original sign on top of Tudor Tower was taken down soon after that building went up.) Although rusted out and unlit for many years (the UN claimed that it was interfering with its communications equipment), the sign had to stay, said the commission, keeping with the requirements that came with historic designation. The board argued that the sign could one day topple down, thinking that might persuade the commission, but the latter counter-argued that the thing was "a piece of real estate history" and thus could not be removed. To rub salt in the wound, the commission told the board that the sign had to be better secured so it wouldn't fall down, an expense that residents were not going to be happy about.[475]

Its relatively minor annoyances notwithstanding, Tudor City has often been recently featured in local newspapers as a highly desirable, not very expensive place to live. In 2005, for example, Patrick O'Gilfoil Healy of the *New York Times* called the community "Brigadoon above the East River," making note of its small-town atmosphere and verdant epicenter. Real-life stories of how apartment hunters fell in love with the place at first glance typically were part of such articles in the real estate or city section of newspapers. Those looking for an affordable co-op more often than not stumbled into the area by chance, these narratives have gone, and were inevitably surprised and delighted by the beauty and isolation of the development. From 7 to 8 percent of the apartments turned over in any given year, creating a constant supply of inventory for new residents to purchase. Tudor City had long been a place to which first-time buyers were attracted because of its reasonable prices, but now apartments were selling for an average of $350,000, not exactly chump change. During the early 1990s recession, studios were going for as low as one-tenth of that number, but prices began to rise as the economy bounced back and as Mayor Giuliani cleaned up the city.[476]

As with New York City real estate in general, prices for an apartment in Tudor City continued to rise over the next decade, but the co-op was still considered a bargain compared to many others because of the usually smaller square footage. As they had always done, longtime residents expressed their passion for the place in a way that was rare and somehow special. Tudor City was "the jewel of Manhattan," said one woman who had lived there for thirty years in 2011, citing the friendliness, proximity to midtown and historic nature as a few reasons she loved the community. The arrival of the United Nations and other international organizations in the area had brought diversity and multiculturalism to Tudor City, another thing she liked about the place. Many younger people, especially single women, had moved in during her three-decade tenure, changing the community's image as a haven for senior citizens.[477] Tudor City remains a place with a high percentage of people who live alone, however, again a function of the petite apartments.[478] The relative affordability of Tudor City and the fact that it is considered a safe community have also led parents to buy "starter apartments" for their young adult children, additional contributing factors for the large number of solo dwellers.

Today, the city within a city remains much like it was when built by Fred F. French about ninety years ago. A good number of current residents work at the United Nations or nearby embassies, giving the community a distinct international flavor. Noise from UN protestors can still sometimes be heard, but otherwise the community is remarkably quiet, just as Mr. French promised. (I sometimes go to bed with the window open, a rare privilege in the city that doesn't sleep.) The two parks are still there, of course, although they have been open to the public for years (while being privately managed), part of the deal made with the city to preserve them. No taxes are paid on the parks, more reason why they will never be viewed as a liability or turned into profit-yielding property.

As it approaches its century mark, Tudor City is indeed an urban Eden, I believe, a sentiment shared by others. "It's a quiet neighborhood built over the busiest street in the world and you would never know it was here," said one resident in 2016 who had lived in Tudor City since 1999, adding that "the people are friendly and you know your neighbors."[479] Many current residents like myself use their studios or one-bedrooms as a *pied-à-terre* versus a primary home. A fair number of residents, if given the opportunity, are combining their smaller apartments to make bigger ones, as owners have first dibs on their neighboring unit if put up for sale. (I'm hoping that my neighbor lists her unit so I can perhaps purchase it in order to increase my square footage from the current Lilliputian 250 to a comparatively whopping 500.)

Some of my fellow residents who have lived for decades in the community are fonts of information regarding the storied past of Tudor City; informal elevator conversations, sometimes in hushed tones, have revealed that there has been a more mysterious side of the complex. These "unauthorized" stories complement the official history reported in the media and found in archives and add a more intriguing and even salacious element to the otherwise rather frumpy image of the development. Many of these tales have to do with the not-very-well-kept secret that midtown business executives ensconced their mistresses in the affordable apartments and engaged in after-work dalliances before catching the train to their families in the suburbs. These stories (which recall the storyline in the great 1960 film *The Apartment*) are no doubt true, adding a selling point to Tudor City that Fred French may or may not have recognized.

Old-timers are also apt to tell stories about some of the more interesting characters who populated Tudor City over the years, such the one about the woman who spent her days viewing the East River with binoculars searching for Soviet submarines. From such stories, it seems as if the community had more than its fair share of eccentric tenants, with some explaining that as a natural result of so many people living in tiny apartments for decades. Ghost stories are also part of the unofficial oral history of Tudor City, I've learned, with residents inclined toward the supernatural convinced that they have seen specters occasionally walking the hallways. If ghosts do exist, I'm not surprised that some of them have decided to reside at Tudor City.

Although Tudor City is still a secret to many visitors to the city and even some diehard New Yorkers—a function of its extreme east location, cul-de-sac layout that discourages traffic and residents' preference to stay under the radar—millions of people around the world have caught glimpses of the buildings and apartments in movies. Scenes from Woody Allen's *Bullets Over Broadway*, Francis Ford Coppola's *Godfather Part III* and, most notably, the first three *Spider-Man* films were shot on the breathtaking penthouse terraces of Windsor Tower. (These apartments, which the French Company was desperate to rent during the Depression, now sell for millions of dollars.) Scenes from *Scarface*, *The Bourne Ultimatum* and *The Peacemaker* were shot right outside the buildings, and as discussed in the third chapter, Charlton Heston lived in one of these penthouse apartments when he was at the top of his game in the 1950s. But the real Tudor City is something far more understated, as any resident will tell you. The opportunity to live in such a beautiful place filled with so many individuals' stories is a lovely thing and a true privilege.

NOTES

INTRODUCTION

1. Rachlis and Marqusee, *Land Lords*, 165.
2. Tudor City was at the forefront of this idea of self-sufficient urban neighborhoods. There was "a new concept of metropolitan life and growth, designed to recapture some of the quiet pleasures of the small town and suburbs for families whose home are within the shadows of the skyscrapers," a 1949 article in the *New York Times* read, with Tudor City having achieved just that a full two decades earlier. The only significant thing that could be said to have been missing from the community was a movie theater. "Island Communities," *New York Times*, May 2, 1949.
3. Rather than be considered open space under the 1901 Tenement House Act, Tudor City's two parks were designated as separate building plots, a distinction that would become critical a half century later. And while many other apartment complexes in the city offered their respective residents some degree of green space, the fact that the Tudor City parks were located in midtown Manhattan made them that much more valuable and worth fighting to preserve.
4. There was also a certain irony that a person who grew up in poverty proceeded in later life to demolish the homes of the poor for financial gain.

5. Mary Frances Shaughnessy, who was deeply involved in the conversion of Tudor City to a cooperative in the mid-1980s, said that one would be hard pressed to see any black people in the community until the arrival of the United Nations at midcentury, and the few whom one might then see were Africans who worked at the organization rather than African American tenants. In addition to the 1948 case discussed in the third chapter (when an African American man visiting a friend was denied use of a passenger elevator at Tudor Tower on two separate occasions), another racist incident occurred in October 1961 when two Ghanaian diners at the Terrace Restaurant in Prospect Tower were mocked for wearing hats while eating. (It was a custom in their country.) "Smudging Our Image," *Tudor City View*, November 1961, 5.

6. Interestingly, Hans Wilsdorf, the founder of Rolex watches, introduced its more affordable Tudor brand targeted to a mass audience at the very same time that French was following the same strategy in real estate. "For some years now, I have been considering the idea of making a watch that our agents could sell at a more modest price than our Rolex watches, and yet one that would attain the standard of dependability for which Rolex is famous," Wilsdorf noted at the time, sounding a lot like French explaining his rationale for introducing a high-quality product designed for a broader audience than his luxury buildings. Tudorwatch.com.

7. New York City Landmarks Preservation Commission, "Tudor City Historic District Designation Report," 75.

8. James Morrison, "Who in the World Was Fred F. French?" *City Journal* (Autumn 1998), city-journal.org.

9. See French and French, *Vigorous Life*, for a thorough if overly flattering biography.

10. "Building Securities," *New York Times*, August 19, 1928, 139.

11. Advertisement, "A FRENCH Stockholder Shares in *All* Profits," *New York Times*, February 7, 1928, 40. Although the French Plan was indeed unique in certain respects and was brilliantly packaged and marketed to the general public, other businesspeople, notably S.W. Straus, had and were continuing to finance projects requiring large amounts of capital by drawing in small investors who would then become stockholders in specific developments. Straus was, in fact, widely recognized as the founder of the mortgage real estate bond, having "floated" such securities as far back as 1909. Straus used his own system to finance some very well-known buildings in New York City, including the Chrysler Building, the Chanin Building, the New York Athletic Club, the London Terrace

Apartments and the Ziegfield Theatre. "Funeral Today for S.W. Straus, Banker, Philanthropist," Jewish Telegraphic Agency, September 9, 1930, jta.org.

12. John Taylor Boyd Jr., "Wall Street Enters the Building Field," *Architectural Forum*, July 1929.

13. Rachlis and Marqusee, *Land Lords*, 167–68.

14. "Fred F. French Dies Suddenly Up-State," *New York Times*, August 31, 1936, 15.

CHAPTER 1

15. Advertisement, "New York's Great Citadel of Quiet," *New York Times*, September 15, 1929, RE8.

16. "Topics of the Times," *New York Times*, December 23, 1946, 22; "Tudor City Opening Marked by Luncheon," *New York Times*, October 1, 1927, 6.

17. New York City Landmarks Preservation Commission, "Tudor City Historic District Designation Report," 4.

18. Rachlis and Marqusee, *Land Lords*, 169.

19. New York City Landmarks Preservation Commission, "Tudor City Historic District Designation Report," 4.

20. "Old Section of Manhattan Being Rebuilt with Apartments," *New York Times*, March 4, 1928, 168.

21. Four such buildings, one on East 41st Street and three on East 43rd Street, survived and are protected as part of Tudor City being declared a historic district in 1988. New York City Landmarks Preservation Commission, "Tudor City Historic District Designation Report," 3.

22. Rachlis and Marqusee, *Land Lords*, 165–66.

23. New York City Landmarks Preservation Commission, "Tudor City Historic District Designation Report," 21. Previous real estate developers, notably Maurice Wertheim, believed that Prospect Hill could make a prime area for apartment buildings as the Grand Central area attracted more businesses. In the early 1920s, Wertheim took an architect to the site, but he was skeptical about the possibilities and the project went no further until French came along. Later, French hired Wertheim to buy plots in Prospect Hill, making one wonder what the latter must have thought given that he likely could have developed the area first. "Three Centuries of Change," *Tudor City View*, May 1953, 10–13.

24. "Tudor City to Rise on 5 East Side Acres," *New York Times*, December 18, 1925, 1.

25. Advertisement, "Poor Fish," *New York Times*, September 19, 1929, 19.

26. "Tudor City to Rise on 5 East Side Acres."

27. Advertisement, "Invest in Tudor City and Profit from the Growth of New York," *New York Times*, November 30, 1927, 33.

28. "Developing the Waterfront," *New York Times*, December 19, 1925, 16.

29. "'Back to East Side'—Slogan of Apartment House Builders," *New York American*, December 27, 1925, W-1.

30. "A Cure for Straphanging," *New York Sun*, December 19, 1925, in "Tudor City," brochure, Fred F. French Investing Company Inc., 1926, FFFCR.

31. "Tudor City," *New York World*, December 19, 1925, in "Tudor City," brochure, Fred F. French Investing Company, 1926; "Tudor City," *New York Telegram*, December 19, 1925, in "Tudor City," brochure, Fred F. French Investing Company, 1926.

32. "Tudor City," brochure, Fred F. French Investing Company, 1926.

33. "Tudor City to Rise on 5 East Side Acres."

34. Advertisement, "And Next Summer Will Be Just as Hot—Keep Cool in Tudor City," *New York Times*, July 21, 1927, 14.

35. Rachlis and Marqusee, *Land Lords*, 171.

36. "Tudor City to Rise on 5 East Side Acres." Gans and his team were able to purchase the one hundred houses at good prices in just thirty-five days despite rumors flying that the buyer was a large railroad company. A much wilder story circulating was that oil had been struck in the neighborhood. "French Got His Tudor City Acres in Thirty-Five Days," *New York Herald-Tribune*, December 29, 1925, in "Tudor City," brochure, Fred F. French Investing Company, 1926.

37. Advertisement, "A City within a City," *New York Times*, April 17, 1927, SM23.

38. "Calls Tudor City Boon to New York," *New York Times*, December 19, 1925, 5.

39. Ibid.

40. See J.H. Burton, "The Save New York Movement," *Buildings and Building Management*, February 1917, 15; "Needle Trades Join in 'Saving' New York," *Dry Goods Economist*, December 20, 1919, 38.

41. "Start Tudor City by Tall Apartment," *New York Times*, June 27, 1926, RE1.

42. New York City Landmarks Preservation Commission, "Tudor City Historic District Designation Report," 24.

43. "Tudor City," brochure, Fred F. French Investing Company, 1928.

44. New York City Landmarks Preservation Commission, "Tudor City Historic District Designation Report," 2, 16–17, 24.

45. "Start Tudor City by Tall Apartment."

46. "Large Frigidaire Order," *Wall Street Journal*, July 29, 1927, 2; "Frigidaire Sells to Chains," *Wall Street Journal*, April 24, 1928, 5; "Large October Gain in Frigidaire Sales," *Wall Street Journal*, November 13, 1928, 11.

47. Advertisement, "In Which the Reid Ice Cream Corp. States," *New York Times*, November 3, 1927, 8.

48. Advertisement, "Frigidaire Breaks All Sales Records," *New York Times*, October 31, 1927, 19.

49. "Start Tudor City by Tall Apartment."

50. "Tudor City Breaks Face Brick Records," *New York Times*, December 27, 1926, 28.

51. "To Set First Steel Today on Tudor City Development," *New York Times*, February 8, 1927, 40.

52. "Tudor City Plans Filed," February 17, 1927, 40.

53. Advertisement, "This Is the Announcement You Have Been Waiting For," *New York Times*, January 28, 1927, 10.

54. Advertisement, "As Serenely Quiet as a Country Night," *New York Times*, October 9, 1927, RE10; see Hood's *722 Miles* for a fascinating history of New York City's subway system and the "els."

55. Advertisement, "You Will Feel Differently Because You Can Sleep Soundly!" *New York Times*, August 4, 1927, 16.

56. Advertisement, "Why Not Sleep as Soundly as You Did in the Country?" *New York Times*, September 11, 1927, RE14.

57. "Tudor City," brochure, Fred F. French Investing Company, 1930.

58. Advertisement, "What We Mean by Economy," *New York Times*, August 4, 1927, 25; advertisement, "Bridging the Gap," *New York Times*, June 3, 1928, RE8.

59. Advertisement, "A New City of Convenience," *New York Times*, February 3, 1927, 12.

60. Advertisement, "Hard Work but You Can't Draw Pay for It," *New York Times*, April 6, 1928, 26.

61. Advertisement, "39 Hours a Month Saved," *New York Times*, February 10, 1927, 14.

62. Advertisement, "Five Minutes Walk from Grand Central," *New York Times*, February 17, 1927, 14.

63. Advertisement, "Why Do You Allow This Loss?" *New York Times*, June 1, 1927, 22.

64. Advertisement, "And Now 2 Hours More Every Day for 18 Teachers...!" *New York Times*, August 17, 1927, 48.

65. Advertisement, "Why It Pays Executives to Live in Tudor City," *New York Times*, June 28, 1928, 15.

66. Advertisement, "Do You Travel 7500 Miles to Business?" *New York Times*, March 3, 1927, 16.

67. Advertisement, "Jostled by 1,500,000 People," *New York Times*, March 10, 1927, 20.

68. Advertisement, "Why Not Avoid Crowded Traveling?" *New York Times*, June 16, 1927, 16.

69. Advertisement, "Don't Mix Business and Football," *New York Times*, September 10, 1929, 16.

70. Advertisement, "About that Lunch Hour Stroll...," *New York Times*, April 29, 1927, 24.

71. "Tudor City," brochure, Fred F. French Investing Company, 1926.

72. "44 Leases Are Made of Tudor City Suites," *New York Times*, March 13, 1927, RE1.

73. "$1,000,000 Loan Is Obtained on Tudor City Blockfront," *New York Times*, May 13, 1927, 41.

74. "Flats in Tudor City Are Renting Rapidly," *New York Times*, June 26, 1927, RE2.

75. See Charyn, *Gangsters and Gold Diggers*, for much more on the history of Broadway.

76. Mackaye, *Tin Box Parade*, 3.

77. "Flats in Tudor City Are Renting Rapidly."

78. Advertisement, "Slow Hanging," *New York Times*, April 26, 1928, 30.

79. "Park for Tudor City," *New York Times*, July 24, 1927, RE2.

80. Sunnyside Gardens, also in Queens, was another neighborhood that was successfully integrating common gardens with housing. New York City Landmarks Preservation Commission, "Tudor City Historic District Designation Report," 15.

81. "Machinery Brings Suburbs into City," *New York Times*.

82. Advertisement, "At Last You Can Play Golf in Manhattan," *New York Times*, September 25, 1927, RE9.

83. "Tudor City Tenants to Have Golf Course," *New York Times*, September 25, 1927, RE23.

84. Advertisement, "Over 265 Families Are Going to Make Their Day 2 Hours Longer…," *New York Times*, August 31, 1927, 10.

85. Advertisement, "During 1928 Invest in Tudor City and Profit by the Growth of New York, *New York Times*, January 2, 1928, 64.

86. "Tudor City Opening Marked by Luncheon."

87. "Renting Conditions on the East Side," *New York Times*, November 20, 1927, W18.

88. "Residential Trend on the East Side Enlarging the River Front Centres," *New York Times*, April 22, 1928, 159.

89. "Old Section of Manhattan Being Rebuilt with Apartments."

90. Ibid.

91. Rose Associates—NYC Rentals, "London Terrace Gardens," londonterrace.com.

92. 201 West 16th Street, 201west16.org.

93. For the definitive account of between-the-wars advertising in America, see Marchand's excellent *Advertising the American Dream*.

94. Advertisement, "Green Trees 3 Blocks from Grand Central," *New York Times*, September 5, 1928, 12.

95. Advertisement, "Where for the Winter," *New York Times*, October 3, 1928, 22.

96. Advertisement, "She's a Nice Girl but She Commutes," *New York Times*, September 24, 1929, 22.

97. Advertisement, "A New and Very Good Reason for Bringing Up Your Family in the City," *New York Times*, January 4, 1929, 52.

98. Advertisement, "Where for the Winter."

99. Advertisement, "How Many Rooms Do You Really Need?" *New York Times*, October 12, 1928, 22.

100. Advertisement, "$75 a Month," *New York Times*, December 4, 1928, 14.

101. Advertisement, "The Greatest Assortment in New York," *New York Times*, June 16, 1929, RE12.

102. Advertisement, "In Tudor City an Apartment Is More than an Apartment," *New York Times*, October 27, 1929, RE4.

103. Advertisement, "Now You Can See Them," *New York Times*, May 7, 1929, 18.

104. "Two More Tall Apartments for Tudor City Development," *New York Times*, March 13, 1928, 50.

105. "Tudor City," brochure, Fred F. French Investing Company, 1926.

106. New York City Landmarks Preservation Commission, "Tudor City Historic District Designation Report," 33, 41.

107. "Tudor City," brochure, Fred F. French Investing Company, 1930.

108. Advertisement, "The Vacant Chair—or Father Is Dining in Town," *New York Times*, June 22, 1928, 48.

109. Advertisement, "A Summer Resort for Those Who Summer in Town," *New York Times*, June 26, 1928, 19.

110. "FRENCH Stockholder Shares in *All* Profits."

111. Advertisement, "How the FRENCH PLAN Multiplies Your Money," *New York Times*, October 5, 1926, 35.

112. "Advertisement, "A New City Is Poured into New York Every Year," *New York Times*, April 20, 1927, 33.

113. Advertisement, "Are You Profiting from the Growth of New York City?" *New York Times*, November 10, 1926, 56.

114. Ibid.

115. Advertisement, "Results Obtained by Stockholders Under the FRENCH PLAN," *New York Times*, September 8, 1927, 56.

116. Advertisement, "Park Avenue Profits to Investors," *New York Times*, May 19, 1927, 39.

117. Advertisement, "How Does the Real Estate Investor Really Make Money?" *New York Times*, January 12, 1927, 31.

118. Mackaye, *Tin Box Parade*, 17.

119. "Three New Houses Enlarge Tudor City," *New York Times*, February 17, 1929, 170.

120. Advertisement, "Announcing Something Entirely New in 1 Room Apartments," *New York Times*, February 26, 1929, 30.

121. Advertisement, "Tudor City—It Will Save You Looking Further for an Apartment," *New York Times*, November 17, 1929, RE4.

122. "New Tudor City Unit to Be 42-Story Hotel," *New York Times*, June 18, 1929, 62.

123. Advertisement, "How a Great Vision Has Developed into an Outstanding Business Success," *New York Times*, June 13, 1929, 39.

124. Advertisement, "Essex House Has Splendid Apartments for the Family," *New York Times*, October 27, 1929, RE6.

125. Advertisement, "Tudor City Offers Apartments to Suit Every Need and Every Purse!" *New York Times*, October 13, 1929, RE4.

126. Advertisement, "The New Essex House Has Family-Size Apartments," *New York Times*, October 20, 1929, RE8.

127. Advertisement, "Windsor Tower: The Latest Achievement in Tudor City," *New York Times*, October 27, 1929, RE3.

128. Advertisement, "Fred F. French Apartments," *New York Times*, October 27, 1929, RE9.

129. Advertisement, "See the East River from the Windows of the Windsor Tower," *New York Times*, November 3, 1929, RE3.

130. Advertisement, "How a Great Vision Has Developed into an Outstanding Business Success," *New York Times*, June 13, 1929, 39.

CHAPTER 2

131. "Pupils of '80s Tell of School Pranks," *New York Times*, January 29, 1932, 19.

132. "Tudor City Adds to Golf Facilities," *New York Times*, March 1, 1930, 37. The miniature golf craze ended in 1930, however, and both courses at Tudor City soon disappeared. "Tudor City Golf Course," *Tudor City View*, February 1965, 12.

133. Williams, *City of Ambition*, 90–93.

134. Advertisement, "Safety or Profits," *New York Times*, January 3, 1930, 32.

135. Advertisement, "A Temporary Investment…for a Permanent Income," *New York Times*, January 9, 1930, 38.

136. Advertisement, "Experts Do the Work—You Share the Profits," *New York Times*, January 21, 1930, 38.

137. Advertisement, "I Share the Profits—but Experts Do the Work," *New York Times*, April 6, 1930, 43.

138. Advertisement, "Standard at Tudor City These Extra Luxuries," *New York Times*, February 26, 1930, 20.

139. Advertisement, "Added Luxuries—but They Don't Add to Your Rent," *New York Times*, March 4, 1930, 13.

140. Advertisement, "For the Young Executive These Tudor City Conveniences," *New York Times*, April 2, 1930, 20.

141. Advertisement, "To the Tenants of the Chrysler Building," *New York Times*, April 16, 1930, 18.

142. Advertisement, "Have You Actually Seen Tudor City?" *New York Times*, June 4, 1930, 56.

143. Advertisement, "This Architect Needed Another Hour in His Day," *New York Times*, April 20, 1930, 154.

144. Advertisement, "Now You Can Get Home to Dinner on Time," *New York Times*, October 14, 1930, 34.

145. Advertisement, "This Answers 4 of Your Questions," *New York Times*, June 11, 1930, 35.

146. Advertisement, "Life at Tudor City Has These Advantages," *New York Times*, June 22, 1930, RE6.

147. Advertisement, "Have You Actually Seen Tudor City?" *New York Times*, August 3, 1930, 136.

148. Advertisement, "Here You Can Have a Pleasantly Furnished Room and Bath for Only $14 a Week," *New York Times*, September 17, 1930, 14.

149. Advertisement, "Come to Tudor City Where Even One-Room Apartments Have 572 Guest Rooms," *New York Times*, July 26, 1931, RE4.

150. Advertisement, "If You're Uncertain About Signing a Lease Live at the New Hotel Tudor," *New York Times*, September 28, 1930, RE9.

151. "Tudor City Grows," *New York Times*, August 10, 1930, RE1.

152. Advertisement, "Now You Can Get an Apartment at Tudor City for $64," *New York Times*, October 24, 1930, 43.

153. Advertisement, "Act Now—A Tudor City Apartment at $64," *New York Times*, October 30, 1930, 8.

154. Advertisement, "Investigate This Offer to Share Hotel Tudor Profits," *New York Times*, November 2, 1930, N11.

155. Advertisement, "Hotel Tudor's Success Makes a Good Investment for You," *New York Times*, November 9, 1930, N9.

156. Advertisement, "1930 Is Economy Year at Tudor City," *New York Times*, November 18, 1930, 22.

157. Williams, *City of Ambition*, 94–95.

158. Advertisement, "Legs Are Still the Cheapest Means of Transportation," *New York Times*, December 9, 1930, 17.

159. Advertisement, "If You Don't Walk to Business You Are Extravagant," *New York Times*, December 14, 1930, RE3.

160. Advertisement, "Tudor City January Specials," *New York Times*, January 13, 1931, 22.

161. Advertisement, "At Tudor City Your Money Buys More—2 Rooms $100," *New York Times*, February 18, 1931, 12.

162. Advertisement, "$109 for a Two-Room Apartment," *New York Times*, March 22, 1931, RE8.

163. Advertisement, "$111 for Two Rooms and a Million Dollar Park," *New York Times*, April 12, 1931, RE6.

164. Advertisement, "The Empire State Building Is Open," *New York Times*, May 1, 1931, 14.

165. Ibid.

166. "'Walk to Work and Be Happy,' Says Best Known Walker," *New York Evening World*, February 18, 1931.

167. Advertisement, *New York Times*, May 5, 1931, 30.

168. Advertisement, *New York Times*, May 14, 1931, 16.

169. Advertisement, "A Friendly Place Should Look the Part," *New York Times*, July 8, 1931, 16.

170. Advertisement, "Old World Charm," *New York Times*, August 30, 1931, RE4.

171. Advertisement, "Tudor City Is Unique," *New York Times*, July 16, 1931, 24; advertisement, "There's a Friendly Sort of Spirit About Tudor City," *New York Times*, July 14, 1931, 30.

172. Advertisement, "Hear Children Laugh in Tudor City," *New York Times*, July 23, 1931, 26.

173. "Fred F. French Dies Suddenly Up-State." Some believe that French actually committed suicide in his swimming pool.

174. Rachlis and Marqusee, *Land Lords*, 191–93.

175. Ibid., 181. See also pages 176–91 for a nice summary of French's attempt to duplicate the success of Tudor City, albeit with federal funding and for a different market, on the Lower East Side with Knickerbocker Village.

176. Williams, *City of Ambition*, 90.

177. Rabinowitz, *Urban Economics and Land Use in America*, 103. Alan Rabinowitz is the son of Aaron Rabinowitz.

178. Rachlis and Marqusee, *Land Lords*, 182–83.

179. Mackaye, *Tin Box Parade*, 122–23.

180. "Richards to Play at Tudor City," *New York Times*, June 16, 1933, 23.

181. International Tennis Hall of Fame, tennisfame.com. Tilden himself played at the courts in a June 1936 exhibition before 1,200 spectators. In between matches, members of the 1936 American Olympic fencing team gave an exhibition with "foils and saber." "Tilden Conquers Barnes," *New York Times*, June 21, 1936, S11.

182. "Whalen Gains Final in Pro Net Fixture," *New York Times*, July 18, 1936, 11.

183. See William, *City of Ambition*, for the definitive account of the intersection of the New Deal and New York City.

184. "Tulips for Tudor City," *New York Times*, January 12, 1936, RE2.

185. "Tulip Show Brings Touch of Holland," *New York Times*, May 13, 1936, 25.

186. Ibid.

187. "Artists Plan Carnival," *New York Times*, June 14, 1936, N10; "Tudor City Art on View," *New York Times*, June 18, 1936, 8.

188. "Tudor City Is Active," *New York Times*, September 20, 1936, RE4.

189. "Rentals Feature Park. Ave. Suites," *New York Times*, October 8, 1937, 43.

190. "50,000 Tulips in Bloom," *New York Times*, May 9, 1937, N4.

191. "La Tulipe Noire Opens Exhibition," *New York Times*, May 17, 1937, 21.

192. "Wins Trip to Europe," *New York Times*, June 22, 1937, 21.

193. "Midtown Gardens Placed on Exhibit," *New York Times*, May 6, 1938, 23.

194. Lee E. Cooper, "Pet Dogs Will Be Outlawed as Tenants in Tudor City and Chicago Model Flats," *New York Times*, October 6, 1937, 45.

195. "Rabinowitz Heads French Company," *New York Times*, May 7, 1937; Farnworth Fowle, "Aaron Rabinowitz Is Dead at 89; Pioneer in Housing Development," *New York Times*, April 4, 1973.

196. "Stockholders Organization," *New York Times*, February 1, 1938, 37.

197. "French Plan Rejected," *New York Times*, February 4, 1938, 33.

198. Williams, *City of Ambition*, 327.

199. Advertisement, "Bachelors Fed Up with Doing Their Own Housework Find the Helpful Services of Tudor City a Real Convenience," *New York Times*, January 18, 1940, 18.

200. Advertisement, "Families Tired of Living Away from City Activities Find Tudor City Right in the Center of Things," *New York Times*, January 23, 1940, 10.

201. Advertisement, "Newlyweds Anxious to Keep within the Budget Find an Apartment in Tudor City a Real Economy," *New York Times*, March 14, 1940, 14.

202. Advertisement, "They're Typical New Yorkers and They Live in Tudor City," *New York Times*, May 9, 1940, 12.

203. Advertisement, "You Couldn't Win Them Away from New York…or from Tudor City," *New York Times*, May 15, 1940, 14.

204. "Tulip Time Despite War," *New York Times*, May 7, 1941, 27; "Spring Festival Held," *New York Times*, May 9, 1941, 12.

205. "Old Tenants Return," *New York Times*, November 16, 1941, RE3.

206. Goldstein, *Helluva Town*, 56. Anecdotal evidence suggests that some GIs and other travelers arriving at Grand Central, Penn Station and the various bus terminals scattered through Manhattan (the Port Authority Bus Terminal didn't exist until 1950) were directed to Tudor City by taxi drivers when seeking some "action." There were enough prostitutes living

in Tudor City during the war to qualify it as a red-light district, according to Mary Frances Shaughnessy, something that tarnished the reputation of the community. In fact, Shaughnessy went further by saying that this rather sordid image of Tudor City actually limited how much rent the French Company could charge because it steered potential renters away from the place. These artificially low figures were frozen by rent control after the war, she continued, something that had long-term financial implications for the French Company and, later, Harry Helmsley. Interview with Mary Frances Shaughnessy of Tudor Realty Services, May 14, 2018.

207. "Tudor City Development Occupies Property Where 'Squatters' Lived in Civil War Era," *New York Times*, February 15, 1942, RE1.

208. "'Village' Houses Attract Renters," *New York Times*, March 19, 1942, 39.

209. "East Side Bothered by Sewer Gas Fumes," *New York Times*, March 22, 1935, 3.

210. "Tudor City Tenants Enjoy Play Areas," *New York Times*, July 26, 1942, RE4.

211. Maurice Foley, "City Apartments Set Renting Mark for Fall Season," *New York Times*, August 9, 1942, RE1.

212. "Sets Rental Record," *New York Times*, October 11, 1942, RE3.

213. Goldstein, *Helluva Town*, 268.

214. "Tudor City Gets 18 New Tenants," *New York Times*, December 16, 1942, 38.

215. "Tudor City Gets More Residents," *New York Times*, May 23, 1943, RE5.

216. Goldstein, *Helluva Town*, 66.

217. "Tudor City Gets More Residents."

218. Goldstein, *Helluva Town*.

219. "…Clothes Needed," *Tudor City View*, August 1940, 9.

220. "…Red Cross Poster," *Tudor City View*, August 1940, 5.

221. "Tudor City's Red Cross Unit Widely Supported," *Tudor City View*, August 1940, 6.

222. See Samuel, *Pledging Allegiance*, for the full story of the World War II bond campaign.

223. "Called to the Colors," *Tudor City View*, May 1941, 22.

224. "…First Aid," *Tudor City View*, September 1940, 9; "Coming Events of the AWVS," *Tudor City View*, September 1941, 11.

225. "AWVS Notes," *Tudor City View*, February 1943, 9.

226. "Festival Proceeds to War Service, Inc.," *Tudor City View*, June 1942, 7, 12; "They're in the Army Now!" *Tudor City View*, August 1942, 8; "And Now for the Navy!" *Tudor City View*, October 1942, 8.

227. "Air Raid Precautions for Tudor City Tenants," *Tudor City View*, January 1942, 10.

228. "Residents Organize for Air Raid Protection," *Tudor City View*, May 1942, 10.

229. "Victim Night," *Tudor City View*, January 1943, 9.

230. "The Hermitage…First to Have 'First Aid' Station," *Tudor City View*, September 1942, 9.

231. "Westchester Residents Look to New York," *Tudor City View*, June 1942, 20.

232. "O.E.M. Asks Tenants' Cooperation in Conserving Essential Materials," *Tudor City View*, July 1942, 20.

233. "Scrap Collection on Prospect Hill," *Tudor City View*, November 1942, 12.

234. "Won't You Help?" *Tudor City View*, August 1942, 16; "Tell It to the Marines!" *Tudor City View*, August 1942, 15.

235. "Give Us Bread, but Give Us Roses," *Tudor City View*, April 1943, 21.

236. Goldstein, *Helluva Town*, 31–32.

237. "Christmas Fetes Getting Under Way," *New York Times*, December 22, 1943, 25.

238. "New Unit Planned on Tudor City Site," *New York Times*, August 31, 1944, 26.

239. Lee E. Cooper, "Tiny Plot which Halted Tudor City Plan Finally Acquired by Fred French Company," *New York Times*, June 22, 1945, 32.

240. Ibid.

Chapter 3

241. "42nd St. Trolleys End Runs Today," *New York Times*, November 17, 1946, 5.

242. "Oldest Resident Dies," *Tudor City View*, September 1946, 5.

243. *Tudor City View*, September 1946, 13.

244. *Tudor City View*, October 1946, 7.

245. "Hail and Farewell!" *Tudor City View*, May 1969, 24.

246. "Have You Lost Anything Lately?" *Tudor City View*, July 1948, 7.

247. "Camera Club to Show War Pictures," *Tudor City View*, September 1946, 11.

248. "Tudor City Forum," *Tudor City View*, January 1947, 22.

249. "The Forum Starts Fall Activities," *Tudor City View*, September 1946, 26.

250. "Tudor City Club," *Tudor City View*, September 1946, 13.

251. Ibid., 6.

252. "Praise the Tudor City Club," *Tudor City View*, January 1947, 11.

253. "One More of the Many Changes for 42nd Street," *Tudor City View*, September 1946, 7.

254. "Street Cars Bow Out," *Tudor City View*, March 1947, 24.

255. In May 1947, Eberle estimated the population as beteen 6,500 and 7,000, "greater than that of all but one city in Nevada and Delaware and of all but three cities in New Mexico." "Post Office to Remain," *Tudor City View*, May 1947, 5.

256. "Tudor City Marks 21st Birthday; Pioneer East Side Deals Recalled," *New York Times*, December 8, 1946, 205. Part of the reason the two biggest meatpackers, Chicago-based Wilson and Swift, each sold out—for a handsome seventeen dollars per square foot—was the decline of kosher slaughtering after the war. Keeping kosher was becoming less prevalent across the country as the children of Jewish Eastern European immigrants assimilated into general society. Peter Kihss, "Our Changing City: Upper and Middle East Side," *New York Times*, July 1, 1955, 23.

257. "Good News for Tudor City Residents," *Tudor City View*, October 1946, 12.

258. "Tudor City Marks 21st Birthday."

259. See Hanlon's fine *A Worldly Affair* for the definitive account of the deal.

260. "Topics of the Times," *New York Times*, December 23, 1946, 22.

261. "Welcome Neighbor," *Tudor City View*, January 1947, 5.

262. "Chairman of Board Hails Choice of UNO," *Tudor City View*, January 1947, 5.

263. "New Zoning Curbs Due Near U.N. Site," *New York Times*, January 23, 1947, 12.

264. "Zoning Change Voted to Protect U.N. Site," *New York Times*, May 2, 1947, 4.

265. "The Landlord States His Case," *Tudor City View*, May 1947, 10–11; "Why So Few Apartments Are Being Built," *Tudor City View*, May 1948, 8–9.

266. "Landlord States His Case."

267. "Why Rental Increases Are Asked," *Tudor City View*, May 1951, 6–7.

268. "Topics of the Times," *New York Times*, September 27, 1947, C14. The "Abattoir's Row" on the west side of Manhattan would remain in business for another decade or so, with cattle drivers often having to dodge automobile traffic in the Hell's Kitchen area.

269. "Tudor City Place," *Tudor City View*, November 1947, 6.

270. Hanlon, *Worldly Affair*, 65.

271. "Action Soon on UN Site," *Tudor City View*, March 1948, 9.

272. Hanlon, *Worldly Affair*, 55–56.

273. "Plans for U.N. Site Arouse Tudor City," *New York Times*, July 22, 1948, 17.

274. "City Proposes to Cut Eighteen Feet from Tudor City Parks," *Tudor City View*, July 1948, 9.

275. "Plans for U.N. Site Arouse Tudor City."

276. "Tudor City Protects Proposed Alterations," *Tudor City View*, August 1948, 5.

277. "Moses the Builder," *Tudor City View*, July 1956, 8.

278. "City to Add Land for U.N. Approach," *New York Times*, December 17, 1948, 34.

279. "We're Licked," *Tudor City View*, September 1948, 5–6.

280. Hanlon, *Worldly Affair*, 68.

281. "UN Rumor Factory Active," *Tudor City View*, November 1948, 5.

282. "The Shape of Things to Come," *Tudor City View*, February 1950, 5.

283. "Want to Bet," *Tudor City View*, February 1949, 13.

284. Hanlon, *Worldly Affair*.

285. "A Happy Omen," *Tudor City View*, November 1949, 5.

286. "United Nations Week!" *Tudor City View*, October 1950, 5.

287. "Holding Up a Glass to the U.N. Secretariat Building," *Tudor City View*, November 1950, 26.

288. Hanlon, *Worldly Affair*, 68.

289. "Christmas Carols," *Tudor City View*, December 1950, 5.

290. "Work on U.N. Approach to Start Soon," *Tudor City View*, January 1951, 7.

291. "Progress on the U.N. Approach," *Tudor City View*, January 1952, 6.

292. Hanlon, *Worldly Affair*, 70.

293. "Hotel Is Rebuffed in U.N. Street Plan," *New York Times*, October 24, 1951, 5.

294. "U.N. Area Buildings Get 'Faces' Lifted," *New York Times*, March 21, 1952, 25.

295. "Regrading for U.N. Called Realty Aid," *New York Times*, January 30, 1952, 9.

296. "$405,000 for Hotel on 42d St. Changes," *New York Times*, March 28, 1952, 4.

297. "$100,535 Is Awarded to Tudor City Hotel," *New York Times*, June 19, 1952, 39.

298. "That Shower of Soot," *Tudor City View*, November 1947, 24.

299. "Face Lifting at the Edison Plant," *Tudor City View*, January 1949, 14.

300. "Manhattan's Monthly Quota of Soot," *Tudor City View*, September 1951, 11.

301. "Negro Wins $1,000 in Exclusion Case," *New York Times*, May 26, 1948, 23. The incident was ironic given that Aaron Rabinowitz and his wife were among the directors of the Tudor Foundation, which had been recently created "for the furtherance of a better understanding between racial and religious groups of the city." "Tudor Foundation," *Tudor City View*, January 1947, 14.

302. Meyer Berger, "Transition Opens New Vistas from the Battery to East 40's," *New York Times*, October 20, 1952, 25.

303. "On that Suburban Trend," *Tudor City View*, April 1953, 12.

304. Lee E. Cooper, "Tudor City Block Gets Apartments," *New York Times*, April 4, 1954, R1; Maurice Foley, "Tudor City Unit Among Latest Apartments Rising on East Side," *New York Times*, May 1, 1955, R1.

305. Advertisement, "Tudor City Tennis Club," *Tudor City View*, September 1946, 4.

306. "Tennis Matches Postponed," *Tudor City View*, September 1946, 13.

307. "Tennis Courts," *Tudor City View*, November 1949, 9.

308. "Riggs Plays 6-All Set," *New York Times*, June 5, 1951, 54.

309. "Attractive Offer Turned Down," *Tudor City View*, October 1947, 26.

310. "New Apartment Building Nears Completion," *Tudor City View*, August 1955, 10.

311. "A $64,000 Question," *Tudor City View*, November 1956, 7.

312. "Tudor City Block Gets Apartments"; "Tudor City Unit Among Latest Apartments Rising on East Side."

313. "Now It Can Be Told," *Tudor City View*, May 1954, 8.

314. Wakefield, *New York in the 50s*, 122–23.

315. "New Apartment Building Nears Completion," 12.

316. "Charlton Heston Interviewed by Ed Morrow," *Tudor City View*, November 1955, 5.

317. "Noise Draws Fire from Tudor City," *New York Times*, June 26, 1955, 55.

318. Ibid.

319. "In the Matter of Soot and Noise," *Tudor City View*, September 1957, 7.

320. "Moses the Builder."

321. "Report on Petitions," *Tudor City View*, November 1957, 8.

322. "Does 'Con Ed' Really Care?" *Tudor City View*, November 1957, 8–9.

323. "Are You Helping to Perpetuate This Begging Nuisance?" *Tudor City View*, September 1958, 5.

324. "Silver Anniversary for Our Tudor City School," *Tudor City View*, November 1955, 7. The school operates today as Preschool of America, one of seven such schools scattered throughout New York City.

325. "The Walt Whitman School Comes to Tudor City," *Tudor City View*, June 1956, 5; "New Junior High School to Open," *Tudor City View*, June 1956, 11.

326. *Tudor City View*, September 1958, 12.

327. "Words of Praise for Tudor City," *Tudor City View*, December 1958, 9.

328. "Expatriates from Suburbia," *Tudor City View*, June 1959, 5.

329. "Neighborhood Changes," *Tudor City View*, June 1959, 7.

330. "Live in Tudor City and Relax," *Tudor City View*, September 1959, 5.

CHAPTER 4

331. "Plan to Build on Parkland Upsets Tudor City," *New York Times*, July 31, 1972, 19.

332. "World Brotherhood, Inc.," *Tudor City View*, March 1960, 5–6.

333. *Tudor City View*, November 1960, 12–13.

334. "A Pedestrian Hazard," *Tudor City View*, January 1961, 5.

335. Hanlon, *Worldly Affair*, 103.

336. "Pedestrian Hazard."

337. "We Wonder Why," *Tudor City View*, May 1961, 5.

338. "Fall-Out Danger or Hysteria," *Tudor City View*, October 1961, 5–6.

339. "Is Your TV Misbehaving?" *Tudor City View*, August 1960, 5.

340. "Pigeon Lovers or Loathers!" *Tudor City View*, August 1961, 7.

341. "Tudor City to Get an Office Building," *New York Times*, August 2, 1962, 41.

342. "U.N. Plaza Gains in 10-Year Span," *New York Times*, January 21, 1962, 228.

343. "Activity Is Brisk Near the River," *New York Times*, November 17, 1963, R1.

344. Glenn Fowler, "Tudor City Sets New Sights with First Office Tower," *New York Times*, May 12, 1963, R1.

345. "Executive Manager Named for Tudor City," *New York Times*, April 25, 1963, 52.

346. "Tudor City Hotel Is Sold to Group," *New York Times*, June 19, 1963, 76.

347. *Tudor City View*, June 1962, 5.

348. *Tudor City View*, August 1962, 6.

349. *Tudor City View*, March 1963, 6.

350. Ada Louise Huxtable, "Bold Plan for Building Unveiled," *New York Times*, September 29, 1964, 45.

351. Steven V. Roberts, "Ford Fund's New Building Has Indoor Woods," *New York Times*, October 26, 1967, 49.

352. "Tudor City's Parking Problem," *Tudor City View*, December 1965, 5.

353. Maurice Isserman, "My First Antiwar Protest," *New York Times*, April 14, 2017, nytimes.com.

354. Maurice Carroll, "3,000 Policemen on Parade Duty," *New York Times*, April 16, 1967, 3.

355. Murray Schumach, "Police Keep Rein on March's Foes," *New York Times*, April 16, 1967, 3.

356. "Turmoil on Tudor City Place," *Tudor City View*, May 1967, 5.

357. Carroll, "3,000 Policemen on Parade Duty."

358. Kathleen Teltsch, "Towers, Parks and Walkways Are Included in Proposal for U.N. 'Campus,'" *New York Times*, April 21, 1968, 78.

359. "That Perennial Rumor Is Going the Rounds Again," *Tudor City View*, June 1962, 5.

360. Rudy Johnson, "Tenants Near U.N. Fight Expansion," *New York Times*, December 8, 1968, 36.

361. Ibid.

362. Ada Louise Huxtable, "Proposed Monument Under Glass at the U.N.," *New York Times*, November 12, 1969, 37; Kathleen Teltsch, "Park Plan Shown at United Nations," *New York Times*, November 29, 1969, 33.

363. "Planners Propose Tudor City Zoning," *New York Times*, April 17, 1969, 26. The Board of Estimate was abolished in 1990.

364. Glenn Fowler, "Tudor City Sold for $36-Million," *New York Times*, June 18, 1970, 47.

365. The law passed under the auspices of Mayor Lindsay was an attempt to incentivize new construction, with the city's landlords agreeing to self-regulation. See "The New York Rent Stabilization Law of 1969," *Columbia Law Review*, January 1970, 156–77.

366. "Tudor City Sold for $36-Million."

367. James F. Clarity, "Neighborhoods: Village of Tudor City," *New York Times*, October 23, 1971, 35.

368. Ibid.

369. Ibid. The hotel's cocktail bar and restaurant seemed to be in a constant state of redesign. The Tudor theme was re-adopted in the fall of 1961, with diners surrounded by sixteenth-century styles and motifs, including castle scenes, banners, escutcheons and the royal trappings of Tudor kings. Wall sconces provided a "semblance of a castle courtyard after sunset," Eberle thought after a recent visit, recommending guests choose the specialty of the house: broiled boneless sirloin steak "a la Henry VIII." "Tudor Restaurant and Cocktail Bar Newly Decorated," *Tudor City View*, October 1961, 5.

370. Martin Arnold, "Tudor City Evicts Woman, 82, Who Forgot the Rent," *New York Times*, November 12, 1971, 37.

371. "Tudor City Residents Here Fight to Save Their Parks," *New York Times*, November 8, 1971, 27.

372. "City Action Opening Tudor City Parks to Public," *New York Times*, January 31, 1974, 26.

373. James F. Clarity, "5 Lawmakers to Oppose Plans to Build in Tudor City Parks," *New York Times*, November 14, 1971, 54.

374. "Plan to Build on Parkland Upsets Tudor City," *New York Times*, July 31, 1972, 19.

375. Ibid.

376. Francis X. Cline, "City Offers Tudor City Alternatives in an Effort to Preserve Parkland," *New York Times*, September 20, 1972, 51.

377. Ibid.

378. "The Tudor City Parks," *New York Times*, October 4, 1972, 46.

379. George Cohen, "Tudor City's Private Parks," letter to the editor, *New York Times*, October 23, 1972, 30.

380. "City Planners Vote to Bar Apartments in 2 Midtown Parks," *New York Times*, November 9, 1972, 51.

381. "Board Preserves Tudor City Parks," *New York Times*, December 8, 1972, 13.

382. "Those Tudor City Parks," *New York Times*, December 18, 1972, 38.

383. The Parkchester was at the time the second-largest apartment development in the country. With more than fifteen thousand apartments, Co-Op City, also in the Bronx, was the biggest.

384. Joseph P. Fried, "Condominiums Sought at Tudor City," *New York Times*, December 23, 1973, 25.

385. "Condominiums Sought at Tudor City."

386. Ibid.

387. "City Action Opening Tudor City Parks to Public Is Voided," *New York Times*, January 31, 1974, 26.

388. "Tudor City Tenants in Protest," *New York Times*, February 11, 1974, 39.

389. "New Law Induces Helmsley to Delay Tudor City Change," *New York Times*, June 17, 1974.

390. "Tenant Rally Asks Rent Control Fight," *New York Times*, December 15, 1975, 39.

391. Phillips-Fein, *Fear City*, 1–3.

392. Ibid.

393. "Tenant Rally Asks Rent Control Fight."

Chapter 5

394. Patricia Leigh Brown, "Chronicling the Romance of Tudor City," *New York Times*, April 6, 1989, C3.

395. David Bird, "Tudor City Volunteers Serve in Strike," *New York Times*, May 12, 1976, 36.

396. "Tudor City Salutes Spring," *New York Times*, May 23, 1976, 35.

397. Carter B. Horsley, "Builder Offers to Swap First Ave. Parks with City," *New York Times*, February 9, 1979, B5.

398. Ibid.

399. Glenn Fowler, "A Public Park Is Offered in Dispute at Tudor City," *New York Times*, April 21, 1979, 25.

400. "Tudor City Residents Rally to Save Community Park," *New York Times*, April 16, 1979, 88.

401. "Public Park Is Offered in Dispute at Tudor City."

402. Ibid.

403. Carter B. Horsley, "Tudor City Tenants Protest Plan for Towers and Win Stay," *New York Times*, May 25, 1980, 32.

404. Ibid.

405. Ari L. Goldman, "Tenants of Tudor City Fighting for Oasis of Trees and Courtesy," *New York Times*, May 27, 1980, 81.

406. Ibid.

407. Ibid.

408. "Tudor City Proposal," *New York Times*, May 28, 1980, 83.

409. Paul Goldberger, "Helmsley Plan for Tudor City Land Swap: Its Pluses and Minuses," *New York Times*, January 26, 1981, 81.

410. Philip K. Howard, "New York, Don't Yield to a Tudor City Swap," *New York Times*, June 6, 1980, A27.

411. "Triage in Tudor City," *New York Times*, May 31, 1980, 22.

412. John McKean, "To Save the Tudor City Parks," letter to editor, *New York Times*, June 30, 1980, A18.

413. "Steps Taken to Preserve Small Tudor City Park," *New York Times*, May 31, 1980, 26.

414. Carter B. Horsley, "Details Released on Plan to Save Tudor City Parks," *New York Times*, June 2, 1980, 81.

415. Ward Morehouse III, "Battle Over Tiny Park Is 'David vs. Goliath' Story," *Christian Science Monitor*, June 3, 1980.

416. Ibid.

417. "New York, Don't Yield to a Tudor City Swap."

418. Ibid.

419. McKean, "To Save the Tudor City Parks."

420. Joana Battaglia, "Save Tudor City Parks and a Playground, Too," letter to the editor, *New York Times*, July 5, 1980, 18.

421. Peter Kihss, "Helmsley Proposal for Office Tower on East River Playground Opposed," *New York Times*, January 22, 1981, B3.

422. Goldberger, "Helmsley Plan for Tudor City Land Swap," 81.

423. Ibid.

424. Edward A. Gargan, "Tudor City Swap Gains Approval of Planning Unit," *New York Times*, February 10, 1981, 81.

425. Ibid.

426. "The Lesson of the Tudor Deal," *New York Times*, February 21, 1981, 22.

427. Andrew Stein, "New York City's 'Tudor Deal' Is Not a Deal Yet," *New York Times*, February 28, 1981, 22.

428. Ibid.

429. Molly Ivins, "Koch, in Reversal, Opposes Tudor City Land Exchange," *New York Times*, March 6, 1981, B1.

430. "Koch Now Expected to Oppose a Swap on Tudor City Parks," *New York Times*, March 5, 1981, B14.

431. "Tudor City's Tenants Get Notice on Plan for Parks," *New York Times*, March 11, 1981, B11.

432. "City Sues to Block Tudor City Project," *New York Times*, March 18, 1981, B6.

433. Joyce Purnick, "Tudor City Parks Exchange Opposed by 2 City Officials," *New York Times*, July 18, 1981, 27.

434. Molly Ivins, "New Plan Drawn Up for Exchange of Land in Tudor City Controversy," *New York Times*, April 10, 1981, B1.

435. "Tudor City Parks Exchange Opposed by 2 City Officials."

436. "Green Light on Tudor Parks," *New York Times*, April 20, 1981, A18.

437. Joyce Purnick, "Mayor Expected to Reject Swap with Tudor City," *New York Times*, January 12, 1982, B1.

438. Joyce Purnick, "Tudor City Parks Again Imperiled by Helmsley's Development Plan," *New York Times*, January 29, 1982, B7.

439. Dorothy J. Gaiter, "City Acts to Block Tudor City Survey," *New York Times*, May 21, 1983, 27.

440. "Developer Curbed on Tenant Notices," *New York Times*, May 25, 1983, B3.

441. Sydney H. Schanberg, "Terror in Tudor City," *New York Times*, May 28, 1983, 23.

442. "Rent Office Blocks Tudor City Towers," *New York Times*, July 30, 1983, 25.

443. "Helmsley Loses Tudor City Ruling," *New York Times*, October 4, 1984, B4.

444. Sam Roberts, "Helmsley, to Quit Rental Market, Tries to Sell Tudor City Buildings," *New York Times*, February 7, 1984, B4.

445. Kirk Johnson, "Tudor City: A Home of Parks, Co-Ops and Acrimony," *New York Times*, November 16, 1984, A29.

446. Dee Wedemeyer, "Major Holdings in Tudor City Are Being Sold," *New York Times*, May 8, 1985, B1.

447. Carol Polsky, "Tudor City Eyes Landmark Status," *Newsday*, December 10, 1985, 37.

448. Ibid.

449. Philip S. Gutis, "Tudor City Residents Near Victory in Battle for Parks," *New York Times*, January 5, 1986, A7.

450. Anthony DePalma, "Tudor City Accord Gives Tenants Two Parks," *New York Times*, May 1, 1987, B1.

451. Jane Gross, "Fight for 2 Parks Won by Tudor City 'Kingpin,'" *New York Times*, May 4, 1987, B3.

452. Ibid.

453. Ibid.

454. Linda Moss, "Tudor City Co-Op Deal Races the Clock," *Crain's New York Business*, August 31, 1987, 14.

455. Carol Polsky, "Battles Flare Over Historic Districts," *Newsday*, August 26, 1986, 19; New York City Landmarks Preservation Commission, "Tudor City Historic District Designation Report," 1.

456. Polsky, "Battles Flare Over Historic Districts."

457. Ibid.

458. Ibid.

459. Beth Sherman, "Old English Charm in Midtown Manhattan," *Newsday*, January 21, 1988, 10.

460. Ibid.

461. Ibid.

462. Ibid.

463. David W. Dunlap, "Tudor City Given Status as Landmark," *New York Times*, May 18, 1988, B1.

464. Michael Moss, "Housing Complex Declared Landmark," *Newsday*, May 18, 1988, 9.

465. "Old English Charm in Midtown Manhattan."

466. New York City Landmarks Preservation Commission, "Tudor City Historic District Designation Report," 2.

467. Dunlap, "Tudor City Given Status as Landmark."

468. "Heraldic Designs on Tudor City Buildings," *Tudor City View*, August 1961, 8–9.

469. Margalit Mannor, "Tudor City: April 1989," Municipal Art Society, New York, Bertha Urdang Gallery, 1989, SASB M1—Art & Architecture Room 300, NYPL.

Epilogue

470. Brad Hamilton, "Tenants' Air War," *New York Post*, May 27, 2007, 14.

471. David Freedlander, "Tudor City: Losing Paradise," *AM New York*, April 24, 2008, 4.

472. Christopher Gray, "Streetscapes/Tudor City Parks," *New York Times*, May 15, 1994, A7.

473. Seth Faison, "John McKean, 85, Tudor City Resident and Tenant Leader," *New York Times*, February 14, 1993, A54.

474. Bruce Lambert, "From Tudor City, Protests Against Noisy Protesters," *New York Times*, May 22, 1994, A6.

475. Christopher Gray, "Landmarks Won't Let a Co-Op Fiddle with Its Roof," *New York Times*, November 26, 1995, 9.5.

476. Patrick O'Gilfoil Healy, "A Place Apart Becomes a Place Discovered," *New York Times*, June 19, 2005, J11.

477. "Tudor City: An International 'Jewel' of NYC," *AM New York*, January 6, 2011, 22.

478. Tim Henderson, "Rise of Americans Who Live Alone Could Pose Problems," *Washington Post*, September 29, 2014.

479. Claire Wilson, "Tudor City: The Peaceful East 40s Enclave that's More than Just Its Architecture," Brick Underground, March 16, 2016, brickunderground.com.

BIBLIOGRAPHY

Burrows, Edwin G., and Mike Wallace. *Gotham: A History of New York City to 1898*. New York: Oxford University Press, 1998.

Cannato, Vincent J. *The Ungovernable City: John Lindsay and His Struggle to Save New York*. New York: Basic Books, 2002.

Caro, Robert A. *The Power Broker: Robert Moses and the Fall of New York*. New York: Knopf, 1974.

Charyn, Jerome. *Gangsters and Gold Diggers: Old New York, the Jazz Age, and the Birth of Broadway*. New York: Da Capo Press, 2004.

Diehl, Lorraine B. *Over Here!: New York City During World War II*. Washington, D.C.: Smithsonian Books, 2010.

Ellis, Edward Robb. *The Epic of New York City: A Narrative History*. New York: Basic Books, 2004.

English, T.J. *The Savage City: Race, Murder, and a Generation on the Edge*. New York: William Morrow, 2011.

French, John W., and Fred F. French. *A Vigorous Life: The Story of Fred F. French, Builder of Skyscrapers*. New York: Vantage Press, 1993.

Goldstein, Richard. *Helluva Town: The Story of New York City During World War II*. New York: Free Press, 2010.

Hanlon, Pamela. *A Worldly Affair: New York, the United Nations, and the Story Behind Their Unlikely Bond*. New York: Empire State Editions, 2017.

Hood, Clifton. *722 Miles: The Building of the Subways and How They Transformed New York*. Baltimore, MD: Johns Hopkins University Press, 2004.

Jackson, Kenneth T., and David S. Dunbar, eds. *Empire City: New York through the Centuries*. New York: Columbia University Press, 2002.

Jeffers, H. Paul. *The Napoleon of New York: Mayor Fiorello LaGuardia*. Hoboken, NJ: Wiley, 2002.

Lewis, David Levering. *When Harlem Was in Vogue*. New York: Knopf, 1981.

Mackaye, Milton. *The Tin Box Parade: A Handbook for Larceny*. New York: Robert M. McBride & Company, 1934.

Mahler, Jonathan Mahler. *Ladies and Gentlemen, the Bronx Is Burning: 1977, Baseball, Politics, and the Battle for the Soul of a City*. New York: Farrar, Straus and Giroux, 2005.

Marchand, Roland. *Advertising the American Dream: Making Way for Modernity, 1920–1940*. Berkeley: University of California Press, 1987.

New York City Landmarks Preservation Commission. "Tudor City Historic District Designation Report." 1988.

Phillips-Fein, Kim. *Fear City: New York's Fiscal Crisis and the Rise of Austerity Politics*. New York: Metropolitan Books, 2017.

Rabinowitz, Alan. *Urban Economics and Land Use in America: The Transformation of Cities in the Twentieth Century*. New York: Routledge, 2004.

Rachlis, Eugene, and John E. Marqusee. *The Land Lords*. New York: Random House, 1963.

Roberts, Sam, ed. *America's Mayor: John V. Lindsay and the Reinvention of New York*. New York: Columbia University Press, 2010.

Samuel, Lawrence R. *Pledging Allegiance: American Identity and the Bond Drive of World War II*. Washington, D.C.: Smithsonian Institution Press, 1997.

Shorto, Russell. *The Island at the Center of the World: The Epic Story of Dutch Manhattan and the Forgotten Colony that Shaped America*. New York: Doubleday, 2004.

Wakefield, Dan. *New York in the 50s*. New York: Houghton Mifflin, 1992.

Williams, Mason B. *City of Ambition: FDR, La Guardia, and the Making of Modern New York*. New York: W.W. Norton, 2013.

Wilson, Earl. *Earl Wilson's New York*. New York: Simon and Schuster, 1964.

Wolfe, Tom. *The Bonfire of the Vanities*. New York: Farrar, Straus and Giroux, 1988.

ABOUT THE AUTHOR

Lawrence R. Samuel is the founder of AmeriCulture, a Miami- and New York City–based consultancy dedicated to translating the emerging cultural landscape into business opportunities. He holds a PhD in American studies and an MA in English from the University of Minnesota and an MBA in marketing from the University of Georgia and was a Smithsonian Institution Fellow. Larry writes the *Psychology Yesterday*, *Boomers 3.0* and *Future Trends* blogs for psychologytoday.com, where he has received hundreds of thousands of hits, and is often quoted in the media. His previous books include *The End of the Innocence: The 1964–1965 New York World's Fair* (2007) and *New York City 1964: A Cultural History* (2014).

Visit us at
www.historypress.com